NADIR SHAH in INDIA

SIR JADUNATH SARKAR

SANAGE
PUBLISHING HOUSE

Paperback: 978-936205807-2
Hardback: 978-936205794-5
eBook: 978-936205815-7

Printed by:

Sanage Publishing House LLP
Mumbai, India

sanagepublishing@gmail.com

Table of Contents

CHAPTER I

INTERNAL CONDITION OF INDIA IN 1738: RISE AND PROGRESS OF NADIR SHAH

Degeneration of Mughal Aristocracy

The invasion of Nadir Shah involved the Mughal Empire in disgrace, spoliation, and dismemberment. It was, however, not a cause of the decline of the Empire but one of the clearest symptoms of the decline. The Persian conqueror merely revealed to the world a fact accomplished long before. He broke the spell under which men had been regarding a gorgeously dressed corpse as a strong man.

How was the work of Akbar and Shah Jahan, Man Singh, and Mir Jumla, thus undone? Why did the seemingly flourishing State of Aurangzeb fall down like a house of cards only 31 years after his death? In reviewing the history of these 31 years, we find first of all a startling decline in the character of the nobility and the efficiency of the army. For this the havoc of civil war was to some extent responsible. In the thirteen years following the death of Aurangzeb, seven bloody battles of succession * had been fought among his descendants in which large number of Princes, nobles and the best soldiers had perished. Equally destructive of officers and men were the armed contests between rival nobles. For instance, the Nizam could confirm himself in the viceroyalty of the Dakhin only after defeating their rivals. For the governorship of Gujarat there were three ruinous encounters in which Shujaat Khan and Rustam Ali Khan fell and Sarbuland Khan was defeated.

* Bahadur Shah two, Jahandar Shah three, Farrukb-siyar one and Muhammad Shah one.

The loss caused by domestic discord among the Mughals themselves was multiplied by the slaughter in operations against rebels like the Sikhs, Jats, Bundelas and Mahrattas and on two occasions against the Rathors. The gaps thus created in the ranks of the martial nobility were not filled by the natural succession of worthy offspring, nor by the rise of new men from the commonalty and recruits from abroad in sufficient number and of the right quality, To the thoughtful student of Mughal history nothing is more striking than the decline of the peerage. The heroes adorn the stage for one generation only and leave no worthy heirs sprung from their loins, Abdur-rahim and Mahabat, Sadullah and Mir Jumla, Ibrahim, and Islam Khan Rumi, —who had made the history of India in the 17th century, —were succeeded by no son, certainly by no grandson, even half as capable as themselves. In reading the huge biographical dictionary of the Mughal peerage (the Masir-ul-umara in 3 volumes of 900 pages each), one frequently comes across such entries as these: "This nobleman (naming a general or minister of the first rank) died in such and such a year; he left two sons who did not attain to much advancement"; or that "he had three sons none of whom did anything worthy of being recorded here.'' Often, while the career of the founder of the family occupies eight or ten pages in this dictionary, his son's achievements are exhausted in half a page and the grandson meets with a bare mention which he earns merely because he is his father's son.

Throughout the Mughal period, the best Muslim recruits for civil administration and war alike were foreign adventures or converted Hindus. The strong and efficient exotics rapidly deteriorated on the Indian soil. Therefore, while the infusion of fresh blood into the nobility from the Indigenous Muhammadan population and the foreign immigrants permanently settled in this country did not take place, the only hope of the continued life and vigour of the Stale lay in the regular flow of the right type of recruits from Bukhara and Khurasan, Iran and Arabia. When this flow stopped, the Empire shrivelled up like a tree cut off from its sap.

Alienation of the Hindus and Shias

Akbar had guarded against this danger by making the first beginnings of the conversion of a military monarchy into a national State, —in effect, though not in constitutional form. He tried to range the Hindu warrior tribes behind his hired foreign troops, as the second and more reliable line of defence for his throne. Under him and his successors, Hindu Rajput soldiers had carried the Mughal banners to the banks of the Oxus and the Helmand in the west and those of the Brahmaputra and the Karnafuli in the east. They had garrisoned the Khaibar Pass, defended Garhgaon against the Ahoms and stormed Chatgaon from the Burmese. But Aurangzeb's attempt to annex Jodhpur on the death of his old servant Jaswant Singh, his invasion of Mewar, his incessant destruction of Hindu temples and his rigorous imposition of the hated poll-tax (jaziya), not only alienated the Rajput clans, but convinced all other Hindu races of India that they had no lot or part in the Mughal State and that for the preservation of their honour and liberty of conscience they must look elsewhere. This was the opportunity of the Mahrattas. This belief, rooted deep in the minds of the Hindu officers and vassals of Aurangzeb, made them indifferent or secretly hostile to their master's cause during his wars with Shivaji and his successors. To the Rajput's and Bundelas, who had so long been the staunchest of supports of the Mughal cause, the Mahratta hero appeared as their heaven-sent deliverer, —a Rama slaying Ravana or a Krishna slaying Kansa. This feeling breathes in every line of the Hindu poet Bhushan's numberless odes on Shivaji. He really voices in smooth and vigorous numbers the unspoken thoughts of the millions of Hindus all over India. At the end of the 17th century, they had come to regard the Mughal Government as Satanic and refused to co-operate with it.

By appealing to this feeling, Baji Rao I easily entered Malwa and then made his hold upon that province good. He united the local Hindu chieftains as well as the neighbouring Rajput's of Jaipur and Mewar with the Mahrattas in an alliance against the oppressors of their common religion (dharma). This point comes out very clearly in Sawai Jai Singh's letter to Nandalal Mandaloi (The Chaudhuri of Indor), after the latter had treacherously caused an immense slaughter of his master's troops by his collusion with the Mahrattas (October 1731): "A thousand praises to you, because you, in sole reliance upon my word and with a view to benefit your dharma, have destroyed the Muslims in Malwa and firmly established Dharma there. You have fulfilled my heart's wishes." [Sardesai, ii. 369.]

In the brief space of thirty-one years after Aurangzeb's death, his successors had to wage war, and more than once, with the Sikhs, Jats, Bundelas, Rathors, Kachhwaha, and Sisodia's. Thus, no Hindu tribe of military value was left on the side of the emperor. In addition to this, the Mahrattas were an open sore which drained the lifeblood of the Empire and steadily reduced its size. The Hindus not only ceased to be loyal vassals or the Later Mughals but became open enemies against whom large forces had to be diverted by the emperor in his day of danger from foreign invasion.

The Persians are the cleverest race among the children of Islam. But they stand aloof from the rest of the Muslim world by reason of their belief in the hereditary right of the Prophet's son-in-law to his succession (khilafat). Their faith of Shia-ism is a heresy in the eyes of the immense majority of Musalmans, including those of Northern India, who are Sunnis. The liberal Akbar, the self-indulgent Jahingir and the cultured Shah Jahan had welcomed Shias in their camps and Courts and given them the highest offices, especially in the secretariat and revenue administration, in which their genius naturally shone most. But the orthodox Aurangzeb had barely tolerated them as a necessary evil. In his reign the Shias felt that they were not wanted by him. Many striking examples of his anti-Shia bias are found in his letters and the anecdotes * about him compiled by his favourite Hamid-ud-din Khan. The populace was still more hostile to these heretics. The proposal of Bahadur Shah to read the khutha with a single Shia epithet, led to a riot at Lahore in 1712. Some years later, at Hasana-bad near the capital of Kashmir, 2,500 Shias were massacred by the Sunnis, [K.K. ii. 870] Thus, to the ambitious and gifted Shia adventurers of Persia, India ceased to be a welcome home, or a field where the highest career was open to their talent.

* Ahkam-I-Alamgiri ed. and tr. by J. Sarkar, sec. iv.

Weak Character of Later Mughals

The decline of the Mughal nobility was mainly due to the decline in the character of the emperor because it is the first duty of a sovereign to choose the right sort of servants and give them opportunities for developing their talent and acquiring experience by instructing and supervising them during their administrative apprenticeship. In his private letters, Aurangzeb frequently complains of the lack of able officers during his reign as compared with the glorious days of Akbar and Shah Jahan: az na-yabi-e-adami-i-kar ah! ah! But the following wise saying of the great Wazir Sadullah Khan, which Aurangzeb himself quotes with approval, is a deserved rebuke to such pessimism; "No age is wanting in able men; it is the business of wise masters to find them out, win them over, and get work done by means of them, without listening to the calumnies of selfish men against them." [Ruqati-i-Alamgiri, No, 46.]

In fact, the deterioration in the character of the Emperors must be held to be the primary cause of the decline in the character of the nobility and the downfall of the Empire, The suspicious watchfulness of Aurangzeb and the excessive paternal love of his successors kept the Princes at Court or caused them to be over-chaperoned in their provincial Governments, thus preventing the development of any initiative or business capacity among them. The heirs to the throne of Dehli in the 18th century grew up utterly helpless and dependent upon others, without any independence of thought, fearlessness in assuming responsibility, or capacity to decide and act promptly. Their intellect and spirits were dulled, and they found diversion only in the society of harem women, buffoons, and flatterers. When such Princes came to the throne, if they were wise, they would leave the entire administration in the hands of able Wazirs, —which provoked factious envy among the other ministers; and if they were foolish, they constantly resorted to intrigue for subverting one too powerful minister only to fall into the hands of another.

The faineant Emperor could not and would not govern the country himself, and yet he had not the wisdom to choose the right man as his Wazir and give him his full confidence and support. He was easily led away by the whispers of eunuchs and flatterers and issued orders for the dismissal of old ministers and provincial governors in the vain hope of getting more money or greater servility from their successors.

Thus, the nobles found that career was not open to talent, that loyal and useful service was no security against capricious dismissal and degradation, that their property and family honour were not always safe in such a Court. Their only hope of personal safety and advancement lay in asserting their independence and establishing provincial dynasties of their own. And such a course was also conducive to the good of the people of the province. They could enjoy peace and prosperity only under an independent local dynasty. For, so long as their rulers were sent from the distant Imperial Court, every succeeding day a new favourite might beg or buy the viceroyalty, come with a new letter of appointment, and try to oust his predecessor. Whether these attempts succeeded or failed, the result was the same: the province was filled with war and the rumours of war, plunder, the withholding of taxes, and the closing of the roads. The history of Gujarat under Muhammad Shah graphically illustrates the point.

Formation of Factions at Court and its effects

When Nadir Shah invaded India, the three highest ministers of State were Asaf Jah Nizam-ul-mulk (the Wakil-i-mutlaq or Regent Plenipotentiary), Itimad-ud-daulah Qamar-ud-din Khan (the Wazir or Chancellor) and Khwaja Asim entitled Samsamud-daulah Khan Dauran (the Amir-ul-umara and Bakhshi-ul-mamalik or Head of the Army). Among the provincial governors the highest (if we exclude the Nizam and the semi-independent subahdar of Bengal) was Saadat Khan Burhan-ul-mulk, the subahdar of Oudh and most prominently in the running for a ministership at Court. Of these, we may leave Khan Dauran out, as he was a carpet knight and Court flatterer, without any administrative capacity or experience. The Nizam had been born in Samarqand and had migrated to India in boyhood to seek his fortune under the Mughal banner. The same was the case with Qamar-ud-din Khan the Wazir, who was his cousin. Saadat Khan was a native of Khurasan and had entered India as an adventurer early in the 18th century. These men could feel no patriotism for India because India was not their patria. They had nothing at stake in this country, no share in its past history, traditions, and culture, no hereditary loyalty to its throne. The Mughal Emperor was merely their paymaster, and if they could make better terms with his enemy, they were not such fools as to reject them out of a sentimental love for a land which merely gave them an excellent field for the display of their undoubted talents and promised them a rich reward. It was only in the succeeding generations that their families became rooted in the Indian soil.

When the Emperor was a sluggard or a fool, he ceased to be the master, and guide of the nobility. They then naturally turned to win the controlling authority at Court or in the provinces. This selfish struggle necessarily ranged the nobles in factions, each group or bloc trying to push the fortunes of its members and hinder the success of its rival groups. The Dihli Court under the Later Mughals was divided between the Turani (or Central Asian) and the Hindustani parties,* both Muhammadans, while the Hindu Rajahs sided with the latter. Each faction tried to poison the ears of the emperor against the Other, thwart its plans, stir up its discontented servants, and even engage in active hostility to it when at a distance from the Court. Rebels could not be opposed with all the armed strength of the Empire; they could always count upon secret supporters or at least neutral make-believe opponents in the Imperial Court and camp.

---

* In the second half of the 18th century the division was between the Irani (Persian Shia) and Turani (Sunni) parties.

This moral degradation of the nobility was accompanied by the intellectual bankruptcy of the bureaucracy and indeed of the entire governing classes. There was no far-sighted leader, not clearly thought-out and steadily pursued scheme of national advancement as under Akbar. No political genius arose to teach the country a new Philosophy of life or to kindle aspirations after a new heaven on earth. They all drifted and dozed in admiration of the wisdom of their ancestors and shook their heads at the growing degeneracy of the moderns.

The Mughal Empire had aimed merely at being a police Government and therefore when it could not do its police function well, when it failed to maintain internal order and external peace, it lost its sole reason for existing. The life of the country had hitherto been held together by the Court. Hence, when the throne was filled by puppets, dissolution took place in the bond that held the people together and co-ordinated their efforts and ambitions. Government ceased and anarchy began.

On the eve of Nadir Shah's invasion, the Jats by their depredations had made the roads near the capital unsafe and hindered trade and traffic. The Mahrattas by their regular annual Incursions at first and their permanent lodgment in the frontier provinces (Gujarat, Malwa and Bundelkhand) afterwards, bled the Empire to death. The production of wealth was stopped not only as the direct result of their extortion and ravage but also indirectly through the discouragement of industry and thrift which such insecurity of property creates.

The frequent civil contests, whether among the princes and nobles or between the Government and rebellious subjects, spread a sense of insecurity among the taxpayers. The peasants withheld the land revenue, which was the mainstay of the Government, and the lower officials evaded delivering their collections. The victor in the contest might crush the defaulting riots and peculating tahsildars and turn them out of house and hold, but by doing so he ruined himself all the same, as his only source of income was gone; he had only swelled the number of desperate, homeless, roving brigands and reduced the area under tillage.

The profuse bounty of Nature to this country, its temperate climate which reduces human want and the abstemious habits of its people, all combined to increase the national income of India throughout the sixteenth and seventeenth centuries. The huge "annual addition to the national stock'' made its way to the hands of the governing classes, —if we leave out the small portion that was intercepted by the trader and the revenue-farmer. The wealth of India was the wonder and 'envy of other nations. But the Mughal Court and Mughal aristocracy had not the sense to ensure this wealth by spending a sufficient portion of it on efficient national defence and the improvement of the people's intellect and character by a wise system of public education. Their wealth only made their weakness fatal to them and tempted the foreign invader by assuring him of a success as easy as the booty was large.

A Government which could not maintain order at home was still less likely to command respect abroad. The weakness of the Central Government was soonest felt in the frontier provinces: Malwa and Afghanistan were not guarded in Strength. The Mahratta occupation of Malwa brought Dihli within striking distance of their arms and Baji Rao in 1737 insulted the capital, pillaged, and burnt its suburbs and returned to his base with perfect immunity. The defencelessness of Afghanistan brought Nadir Shah to India.

Decline of the Safawi monorchy and Afghan usurpation of Persia

The Safawi dynasty founded by Shah Ismail at the beginning of the 16th century, freed Persia from foreign rule and the wars of domineering nomad tribes. The new line of kings gave the country peace, prosperity, and extension of territory. The faith of the people, which had been persecuted by the former rulers as a heresy, now became the State religion. Wealth and civilization increased, and Persia again took her ancient position as one of the world's famous and independent monarchies, the rival of Turkey, and Hindustan, in the eyes of the Muslim world.

For nearly a century and a half after the founder, a succession of wise, warlike, and active kings maintained the strength and glory of Persia. But about the middle of the 17th century began the inevitable decline in the monarchy from a continuous decline in the character of the monarch. In the words of the historian Sir John Malcolm, during the century following the death of Abbas the Great (1627), the Persian throne was occupied by "a succession of weak, cruel and debauched monarchs The lower orders became every day more unwarlike and ceased to be able to defend the State....The nation may be said to have existed on the reputation it had acquired before." [Hist, of Persia, 2nd ed., i 379.]

Shah Husain, the last of the Safawi line, who reigned from 1694 to 1722, was no doubt free from vice but he went to the opposite extreme of meekness and religious bigotry and did still greater harm than his dissolute predecessors. He placed the administration entirely in the hands of the priests and thus alienated the old martial and official nobility. Under the advice of the keepers of his conscience, the king persecuted and banished from the land the Sufi Philosophers as heretics from Islamic orthodoxy and thus enraged the intellectual classes. But the prestige of his worthier ancestors had given the state a momentum which made it continue to go on for nearly twenty years longer.

At last, early in the 18th century the dissolution came and from the hands of its Afghan subjects. Ever since Abbas I's conquest of Qandahar early in the 17th century, Southern Afghanistan had been a province of Persia, it was the home of the Ghilzai and Abdali tribes. The wise statesmanship of the earlier Shahs had left the subject races of the Persian Empire under their own laws, and often under their own magistrates. The turbulent character of the Afghan people, the wildness of their country and their position on the debatable land between the rival monarchies of India and Persia, enabled them to extort for themselves a considerable amount of local independence. Their submission to the Central Government was lax and dependent on their own pleasure. In 1708, a new Persian governor of Qandahar, the converted Armenian Gurgin Khan, by trying to rule with a strong hand, caused an explosion. The Ghilzai tribe rose under Mir Wais, killed the governor, seized Qandahar, and established their own rule there.

The successful rebel's son Mahmud gained the throne of Qandahar in 1717 and led his tribe on to the plunder of the effete king and people of Persia. The Safawi Empire now broke to pieces. Mahmud captured the capital Isfahan and on 21st October 1722 Shah Husain Safawi resigned his ancestor's throne and the Afghan rule over Persia began. Mahmud was succeeded by his uncle's son Ashraf in 1725. But new dangers threatened the conquerors. Qandahar was held by Mahmud's brother, whom Ashraf could not oust from the fort. Thus, the Ghilzai tribe became divided under two chiefs reigning at two distant places. The governor of Sistan annexed nearly all Khurasan and proclaimed his independence. But Ashraf's greatest enemy was Mirza Tahmasp, the son of the deposed Shah Husain, who had assumed the royal title and was trying to establish his power in the province of Mazendran. This Prince was a foolish, effeminate, and debauched youth and could not have recovered his heritage by his own efforts. But he was now joined by Nadir Quli, the greatest Asiatic general of that age. [Malcolm, i. 401-465.]

Nadir delivers Persia and makes Himself King

Nadir Quli was the son of Imam Quli, a poor Turkoman of the Afshar tribe long settled in Khurasan, who earned his bread by making coats and caps of sheepskin Nadir was born in 1688 and passed his early years amidst great hardship and privation, which only called forth his extraordinary genius and energy. He was carried away to Tartary by the Uzbak raiders and kept there as a prisoner for four years. On returning home he served under some petty chiefs and finally took to a life of robbery with his own band of hardy and adventurous followers. The eclipse of Government during the Afghan usurpation of Persia enabled him to pursue such a career with safety and much profit in the ill-controlled frontier province of Khurasan, Seizing the fort of Kalat by murdering his own uncle (who was its governor), he used the power thus gained to defeat the Afghan ruler of Khurasan and recover the city and district of Naishabar. This victory in the national cause secured his welcome by his lawful king Shah Tahmasp, whose service he entered in 1727. [Malcolm, ii 25; M.U., i. 823.]

The fame of Nadir drew the best recruits to his side, and he became the centre of the Persian national effort to throw off the foreign yoke. His genius for war and diplomacy and his concentration of all authority in his hands led to his rapid and unbroken success. Persia was recovered from the Afghans, very few of whom returned to their own country from the slaughter on the battlefield or murder at the hands of the 'incensed peasantry. The Afghan domination had been a seven years' horror to the afflicted people of Persia. "Within seven years nearly a million of her inhabitants had perished, her finest provinces had been rendered desert, and her proudest edifices levelled with the dust; and this by enemies who had neither the force nor the wisdom to maintain the conquest." [Malcolm, i, 472.] The national deliverance of Persia was the work of Nadir alone, and naturally the enthusiasm of the people for him was unbounded. The king showed his gratitude by granting to the general half the kingdom with a richly jewelled crown and the right of stamping coins with his name.

But during Nadir's absence in the eastern provinces, the king, who had injudiciously conducted expeditions in the West, lost his general's gains in that direction and made a humiliating peace. The national indignation was very great. The officers of the army felt that if Shah Tahmasp were left at the head of affairs, he would only undo all their recent work and bring back national servitude. They with one voice urged Nadir to assume the crown. [Anandram, 34 Malcolm, ii. 8—II.] But though Tahmasp was deposed, 26 August 1732, his general did not as yet venture to sit on the throne. Abbas, an eight-month-old son of Tahmasp, was proclaimed king and Nadir became his regent with full authority. Four years later the infant died, and Nadir became king with the title of Shahan Shah Nadir Shah, 26ih February 1736.

He wrested Armenia and Georgia from the Turks and made a peace with the Russians by which he gained the lost provinces bordering the Caspian. The island of Bahrain was recovered from the Arabs. Next, the predatory Bakhtiari tribe of the Shuster hills was vanquished and enrolled in his army, —thus diverting their energies into a useful channel and keeping them from disturbing the peace [Malcolm, ii. 11-18,]

Finally, early in 1737 Nadir Shah started with 80,000 men against Qandahar, So, long as that centre of independent Afghan power was not destroyed, it would remain a menace to the safety of Persia and constantly disturb the peace and prosperity of Khurasan. Moreover, without the conquest of Qandahar the full heritage of the Safawis could not be said to have come into his possession. This fort stood on the route of his advance to the Mughal Empire, and he wished to enlist the Afghans under his banners to assist him in his foreign conquests, as Mahmud of Ghazni had done seven centuries before.

Qandahar was now in the possession of Husain, the younger brother of Mahmud (the usurping king of Persia). The old city * stood on the eastern slope of a ridge, two miles west of the modern city. Its walls were of extreme strength and the garrison had made preparations for a good defence. The Persian army invested it on 30th March 1737, but the siege dragged on for a year and the fort fell ** only on 12th March 1738. The fort and city were dismantled by the victor. In its environs he built a new city with quarters for the governor and soldiers, which was named Nadirabad by him but is now known as modern Qandahar. He treated the defeated Afghan tribesmen very kindly, released all the prisoners taken, bestowed pensions on the tribal chiefs, enlisted the clansmen in his army and by transplanting the Ghilzais to Naishabur and other places in Khurasan (the former homes of the Abdalis) and posting Abdali chieftains as governors of Afghanistan (Qandahar, Girishk, Bist and Zamin-dawar), kept his former enemies usefully employed in his service. His policy was to tempt the other Afghan forts to surrender to him by creating a reputation for himself as a merciful enemy and liberal head and to enlist the Afghan soldiers under his banners as devoted supporters of his projected conquests of Central Asia and India. [Jahankusha, 311-328; Malcolm, ii. 20; Anandram, 6-8.]

* For a description of the fort and its walls, see J. Sarkar's History of Aurangzib, i 140-143.

** Anandram, P. 7, says to treachery.

After the fall of Qandahar came the turn of the Mughal Empire and here Nadir made out a strong case for declaring war. He proceeded in such a way as to ensure that neutral States and lovers of international law would not be able to condemn his invasion of India as an act of wanton aggression and spoliation. Nadir was no mere soldier, no savage leader of a savage horde but a Master of Diplomacy and statecraft as well as of the sword. The profoundness of his diplomacy was no less remarkable than the greatness of his generalship in war and the wisdom of his policy to the vanquished after his victories in the field.

Causes of the Diplomatic Rupture between the Persian Government and the Mughal Empire

The conduct of the effete Court of Dihli towards Persia had been marked by violation of diplomatic usage and courtesy and even by unfriendly negligence. For several generations past there had been an exchange of envoys, presents and diplomatic courtesies between the Mughal Emperors of India and the Safawi Shahs of Persia. Abbas 11 continued this practice even after he had wrested Qandahar from Shah Jahan and fought four campaigns against Mughal arms. At all events, formal letters of congratulation used to be written by the one Court to the other at every new accession to the throne. But Muhammad Shah, forgetting this usage, neglected to felicitate Shah Tahmasp TI after he had overthrown the Afghan usurper and recovered the throne of his ancestors. Nay, the Dihli Government, no doubt out of a timid love of quiet, had kept up friendly relations with Mir Wais and his son Husain (The usurpers of Qandahar), though the latter had raided the province of Multan and ravaged the imperial territory.

After the expulsion of the Afghans from Persia, Nadir had sent Ali Mardan Khan Shamlu as ambassador to India to inform the Dihli Court that a campaign against the Afghans of Qandahar would be soon undertaken, * and to request that the emperor would order his subahdar of Kabul to prevent these Afghans from escaping into his territory. Muhammad Shah replied that he had issued instructions to this effect and would reinforce the army in Kabul to have this work done.

* Ali Hazin says that Shah Tahmasp II, after recovering Isfahan, sent one of his nobles to India as envoy to report his accession and to request Muhammad Shah to keep the Ghilzais out of his territory and that after the accession of the infant Abbas III, a similar message was sent. But Jahankusha 331, shows that both these embassies were sent by Nadir.

After some time, Nadir sent a second messenger, Muhammad Ali Khan, with a similar request and the Dihli Government replied in the same terms. When early in 1737 the Persians invested Qandahar and the local Afghans began to flee northwards into Mughal Afghanistan, Nadir despatched a force to Ulang Muragha, in the Qalat district, which was his last outpost on the Perso-Mughal frontier, to bar the path of the retreating Ghilzais. This detachment ravaged the country up to the end of the hills of Kalat, slaying about a thousand Ghilzais and capturing much booty and many prisoners. The rest of the tribe fled into Mughal territory, towards Ghazni and Kabul, there being no Mughal officer or army on the frontier to obstruct them. The Persian generals, not having received orders to cross the frontier, stopped there and reported the affair to their master. Nadir Shah then (30th April 1737) sent a third envoy, Muhammad Khan Turkoman, to India by way of Sindh, to ask for an explanation of this breach of promise on the part of the emperor. The messenger was ordered to spend no more than forty days in India but bring a reply within that period. The Dihli Court, however, would give him neither a reply nor the permission to return. Its imbecile policy is thus described by Ali Hazin: "As soon as this envoy arrived at Shahjahanabad, he delivered his letter and was told to wait; but they were silent as to any answer. Sometimes they were unable to agree in their own minds on the question of writing any answer at all; at other times they were perplexed [as to] what titles they should use to Nadir Shah.... Thinking the detention of the ambassador a stroke of State policy, they waited to see, if perchance Husain the Afghan with the troops besieged in Qandahar gained the victory over Nadir Shah and destroyed him or put him to flight; on which event there would be no need of writing any answer to his letter."

A year passed away in this way and then after the fall of Qandahar, Nadir wrote to his envoy in India to return at once. The matter had passed beyond the stage of correspondence and discussion. Nadir had decided on invading India. [Jahankusha, 331-332; Belfour's AH 281-287 (which is paraphrased in Siyar, i. 93-94)]

Neglected and defenceless condition of Afghanistan and the Panjab

At this point it is necessary to stop the narrative of events and look at the condition of the provinces forming the Northwestern frontier of the Mughal Empire. Afghanistan had been a precarious possession and source of weakness to the successors of Babar, but they had succeeded in occupying the country and keeping the passes from India open. The earlier Mughal Emperors had repeatedly visited Kabul. But during the long reign of Aurangzeb, the imperial authority there was seriously imperilled. The formidable rebellion, first of the Yusufzais of Peshawar (1667) and then of the Afridi's of Khaibar (1672), was aggravated by a rising of the Pathan population along the entire North-western frontier against the ruler of Dihli. The resources of the whole Empire had to be concentrated under the emperor's personal command against the tribesmen. After only a modified success Aurangzeb returned from the frontier where he had now spent two years and peace of a sort was restored by profuse bribery to the border Afghans (1676), Next year Amir Khan * was appointed governor of Kabul and he held the post for 21 years with conspicuous ability and success. Aurangzeb ascribes this viceroy's administrative triumph to his tactful dealings, practical skill, policy of keeping the hillmen usefully employed by enlisting them in the imperial army, and his judicious and economical management of the treasury, which enabled him to pay regular subsidies to the clansmen living near the passes.

* See J. Sarkar's History of Aurangzib, iii. (2nd ed.) 243 and Studies in Mughal India, III—117.

When Amir Khan died (1698), he was followed by no worthy successor. After a short lull, trouble began to revive. But Shah Alani, who governed the province from 1699 to his father's death in 1707, kept order fairly well. He had a large and efficient army and used to move about the country a good deal, passing the winter at Peshawar (which was then included in Afganistan) and the summer at Kabul or Bamian but he was forced to continue the policy of bribing the pass Afghans to maintain peace. In 1709 or 1710, Nasir Khan, formerly faujdar of Jamrud, was appointed subahdar of Kabul, and he continued to hold this post till his death, about 1719, when his son, also entitled Nasir Khan, succeeded him, and was later confirmed in his office by Muhammad Shah (1720). This second Nasir Khan's mother was of the Afghan race, and he was expected to succeed easily in ruling the province and keeping the passes open. [M.U. 111, 833.]

But he was a simple-minded and indolent man. His chief business was hunting and when not engaged in it he spent his time in prayer, [Siyar i. 93.] Thus, the peace of the country was left to take care of itself, and the roads became unsafe. His patron at Court was Roshan-ud-daulah, a favourite of the emperor and the imperial grant for payments to keep the passes open was sent to Nasir Khan through the hands of this noble. Roshan-ud-daulah's rival Khan Dauran accused him of embezzling the money and induced the emperor to stop this payment as useless. Nasir Khan's appeals were disregarded. About 1730 Roshan-ud-daulah himself fell out of favour and was dismissed; the result was that things in Afghanistan were left to drift without the least hope of remedy.

As Ghulam Husain writes, "Neither the subahdar nor the Amir-ul-umara (at Court) kept himself informed about the roads and passes of the country. No guards remained on the roads. Owing to the weakness of the Government, the local officers lost all fear of being called to account. None cared for anyone else, none feared, none sought instructions from any (higher officer), Everywhere everyone did whatever he liked. Anyone who wished could come and go [through these frontier roads, unquestioned]: the emperor, and his nobles never heard of it. They never inquired why no newsletter was coming to Court from any province or outpost." [Siyar, i. 93.]

When we contrast this negligence and slothfulness of Muhammad Shah with the sleepless vigilance * of Aurangzeb in respect of the Persian frontier, we can realise the depth of inefficiency to which the Mughal administration had fallen on the eve of Nadir Shah's invasion.

---

* Striking illustrations in Hamid-ud-din's Ahkam-i-Alamgiri 49-52, translated by J. Sarkar as Anecdotes of Auraugzib.

The governor of Kabul had sent repealed applications to the emperor for money to pay his troops, but nobody paid any heed to them, as the faction opposed to him was now in power at Court and the Emperor never exercised his own judgment nor personally looked into any business. The soldiers posted in the province starved as their salary for five years was in arrears. ill-fed, ill-equipped, ill-armed through poverty, they pressed the subahdar to pay them at least one year's dues out of the five, so that they might satisfy their creditors to some extent and have a little left over for the expenses of marching. Nasir Khan used to reassure them by saying, "Friends! why this anxiety? I have written to the emperor and also to my agent at Court, and the money is sure to come tomorrow, if not today." When his agent presented the application to Khan Dauran, the Amir-ul-umara and in fear and trembling, described the alarming situation in Afghanistan, that noble replied in derision, "Do you think that I am a petty simpleton that I shall be impressed by such a tale as yours? Our houses are built on the plain; we do not fear anything except what we can see with our own eyes. Your houses stand on lofty hills and therefore you have probably sighted Mongol and Qizilbash armies from the roofs of your houses! Reply to your master that we are writing for money to the governor of Bengal and when the Bengal revenue arrives after the rainy season, the money due will be quickly sent to Kabul." * (Anandram, 11-12.)

Those people of Dihli who bore testimony to the defenceless condition of Afghanistan were sneered at as fools. Khan Dauran's friends even suggested that the deputation of Kabul citizens with this report had been stage-managed by the

Wazir and the Nizam (the leaders of the Turani faction) in order to discredit Khan Dauran and induce the emperor to transfer his confidence to the former party! [Siyar, i. 96.]

---

* On this Anandram rightly remarks: "If the Afghans had been set to guard the frontier with their whole hearts and customary bravery, they could have stopped the advance of the Persian army long enough to enable reinforcements to reach them from Dihli, and then India would not have been sacked."

The result is best described in the words of Ghulam Husain: "It was impossible for Nasir Khan to prevent Nadir Shah's entrance into India, The Government was rotten, the emperor was powerless. No money was sent to maintain the administration in Afghanistan. The Subahdar, therefore, sought his own comfort and lived at Peshawar, entrusting the fort of Kabul to a qiladar with orders to control and watch the passes leading into India." [Siyar, i. 94.]

Equally neglected and defenceless was the next gateway of India, the province of the Panjab. Zakariya Khan (son of Abdus Samad Khan) was the governor of Lahore and Multan. His family had come from Ahrar in Central Asia and therefore he was regarded as "a strong pillar of the Turani party." His mother was a sister of the late Wazir Muhammad Amin Khan's wife and he naturally, excited the bitter opposition of the Hindustani party under Khan Dauran. *Zakariya Khan was a brave and active soldier and good administrator; he gave peace and prosperity to the province in his charge by repeated campaigns against rebels and robbers. [M, U. ii, 106; Anandram, 138.] But the Hindustani party who possessed the emperor's ears, opposed all his applications to court, misrepresented his character and motives and prevented money and troops from being sent to him when Nadir's invasion was imminent.

---

* An astonishing example of this party rancour is supplied by the historian Shakir Khan (an Indian Muhammadan of Panipat), who asserts that Zakariya Khan at the instigation of the Nizam and Saadat Khan, who wanted to overthrow Khan Dauran, disloyally admitted Nadir into Lahore!

Thus, in the emperor's hour of supreme need, factious jealousy and foolish distrust prevented any real attempt being made to repel the invader from the frontier or even to check him there long enough to enable defensive preparations to be completed at Dihli and the army of the Empire marshalled in the Panjab. The 'gateways of India' fell into Nadir's hands at the first touch and yet the foolish Emperor and his advisers delayed their own preparations for defence in the vain hope of the enemy not being able to force the passes of Afghanistan and the rivers of the Panjab.

Such was the condition of the north-western marches of India when the storm burst on them.

Nadir conquers Northern Afghanistan from the Mughals

On 10th May 1738, the Persian monarch began his march into Northern Afghanistan to make an end of his Afghan enemies. Crossing the Mughal frontier at the Mukhur spring, he halted at Qarabagh, 36 miles s.w. of Ghazni. A powerful detachment was sent under his younger son Nasr-ullah to operate against the Afghans of Ghorband and Bamian in the north-west of Kabul. When Nadir reached Qarabagh, Baqi Khan the Mughal governor of Ghazni fled away in terror; the Qazi's, scholars and rich men of the city waited on the invader with presents and offer of submission. So, he entered Ghazni in peace, 31st May and treated the people well.

Two other detachments had been operating against the Hazaras or hill Afghans, south-west of Ghazni, who had defied Nadir's troops. All who made timely submission were pardoned. But the men who resisted were put to the sword, their women dragged into captivity and their houses destroyed. Thus, securing his flank and rear, Nadir advanced on Kabul. The chief men of the city tried to avert the storm by advancing two marches to welcome him on the way and he sent them back with robes of honour, presents and reassuring words. But Sharza Khan, the commandant of the citadel, with the soldiers of the garrison decided to offer resistance and shutting the fort-gales, prepared for defence.

On 10th June, Nadir's advance tents arrived near the fort, but a part of the garrison sallied out and made a hostile demonstration. The porters were not prepared for resistance and therefore, declining the challenge, they quietly set up the tents at a safe distance from the walls, at Ulang, half league to the east of the city. Nadir arrived here on the 11th and next day he rode out towards the Black Rock to view the environs of the city and the defences of its citadel. The garrison issued in force and began to discharge their firearms at him; but a charge of the Persian escort drove them back to the foot of the wall. Nadir now began an investment of the city. His guns and mortars, dragged up to the neighbouring heights, played upon the walls. On the seventh day (19th June) the tower of Aqa-bin collapsed from the shock of a big gun fired from it and a part of the wall* fell down; the citadel capitulated and the Imperial treasury, horses, elephants, and stores at Kabul passed into Nadir's possession. [Jahankusha,333-335.]

*Anandram 10. He tells the incredible story that the breach thus caused was large enough to let 500 horsemen gallop through it abreast. The recoil of a single gun could not have overthrown a quarter mile of stonewall. Hanway (ii. 359) say that Nadir massacred the greater part of the garrison including Sharza Khan and his son, after the fall of Kabul.

Here he passed forty days to settle the affairs of the province and here he was joined (1st July) by his son Nasr-ullah who had returned after subduing Ghorband and Bamian. In the meantime, a letter had been received from his envoy at Dihli reporting that the emperor would neither reply to his letter nor give the ambassador his conge. At this Nadir Shah wrote a strong protest to the emperor and sent it with a fast courier accompanied by some leading men of Kabul, who offered to explain the real state of things in Afganistan to the Mughal Court. In this letter Nadir Shah charges Muhammad Shah with the violation of his promise, delay in replying to embassies and detention of the last Persian envoy for more than a year, in violation of the usage of nations. He points out how the Afghans had done even greater havoc to India than to Persia and therefore in crushing them he was really doing a service to the Mughal Empire. He explains how the hostility of the imperial garrison in Kabul and their alliance with the Afghans had forced him to fight them but that after their submission he had guarded them from harm, as his sole intention was the punishment of his Afghan enemies. The party entrusted with this letter left Kabul on 3rd July. On their reaching Jalalabad, the Kabuli notables were forced by the local governor to go back, while the courier and his nine guards were robbed and murdered by a neighbouring chieftain, the son of Mir Abbas.*

*Jahankusha,335—337, Ali Hazin, 288.

Meantime Nadir Shah had left Kabul (19th July) on account of scarcity of provisions there and moved into the more fertile and populous hills of Chahar-ek-kar Najrad and Safi. The hillcrests occupied by the local clansmen were stormed and the vanquished were forced to submit and enter the Persian military service. After passing 22 days here, he started for Gandamak on 25th August.

Then came the news of the murder of the courier. The Persian advanced guard made a sudden dash on Jalalabad and seized the grain stored there. The governor fled, the chief men submitted and yielded up the fort (7th September). But the city was subjected to a massacre in punishment of the attack on Nadir's courier. The hillfort of Mir Abbas's son was stormed, the men were put to the sword and the women (including his sister and wives) were brought away to the Persian camp as captives. [Jahankusha, 337—339, Ali Hazin, 289.]

After spending some days in regulating the administration of the country, the Persian king advanced to Bahar-Showlani† to the south of Jalalabad. In view of his expected long absence in India, the distance of Dihli from his base in Persia and probably also the accidents of war, Nadir Shah invested his eldest son Mirza Raza Quli with the crown of the deputy-king or regent of Persia (3rd November) and sent him back to that country amidst great pomp at the head of a strong force.

† Bahar 17 m. s. w. of Jalalabad; Showlani (spelt Safli in Jahankusha) 8 m.e. of Bahar.

CHAPTER II

NADIR SHAH'S INVASION OF INDIA: NADIR SHAH CAPTURES PESHAWAR AND LAHOR.

On 6th November 1738, the march towards India was resumed. The main army under Nadir Shah passed Jalalabad on the 12th and halted a mile beyond it. From this stage a vanguard of 12,000 picked cavalry proceeded ahead, followed by another body of 6,000 men to guard the royal tents. Then came the Centre and the Rear.

Nasir Khan, the Mughal governor of Afghanistan was according to his usual custom, living at Peshawar when he heard of Nadir's conquest of Kabul and projected invasion of India. He assembled some 20,000 Afghans of the Khaibar and Peshawar districts and blocked the pass between Ali Masjid and Jamrud, — the last outpost being 12 miles west of Peshawar. His half-starved soldiery and hastily raised tribal levies were in no condition to oppose the Persian veterans flushed with a hundred victories and led by a heaven-born general.

In the afternoon of 14th November, after the asar prayer, Nadir Shah left his camp and baggage at Barikab (20 m. east of Jalalabad) under Nasr-ullah Mirza and made a rapid march with light kit by the Seh-chuba route. Though the path was steep and extremely rough, he covered fifty miles before eight o'clock next morning and fell upon the Indian army in the Khaibar Pass most unexpectedly from the flank. One charge of the Persians scattered Nasir Khan's raw levies; but he resisted with his regular troops for some hours; in the end he and several other nobles were captured; * the rest of his army fled, leaving their entire camp and property in the hands of the victors. [Jahankusha, 341-342; Ali Hazin 290.]

---

*Mahdi says that Nasir Khan drew up his troops in line of battle and resisted the Persians for some time. Siyar (i. 95) says that this general was captured, wounded, and then revealed his name and rank. Anandram (13) asserts that Nasir Kh. was surprised while asleep in bed and fled in confusion with Chiragh Beg Khan and a few other attendants. Hanway (ii. 362) tells us that Nadir bought over the pass Afghans whom the Dihli Court had kept in arrears for 4 years and thus he could cross the pass easily and unopposed. Nasir Khan deserted by his raw levies at the unexpected approach of Nadir, entrenched himself near Peshawar with 7,000 men and fought for some hours but his lines were stormed, and his men slain or captured. Ali Harin (290) says that an immense crowd of the Afghans and of Nasir Kh's troops were cut to pieces in the valley.

Three days after the victory, the Persian camp and rearguard arrived there by the regular road. On 18th November Nadir entered Peshawar without opposition and occupied the governor's palace. On 12th December the advance was resumed. A strong column under Aqa Muhammad was sent ahead to raid and ravage the country and build a bridge over the Indus at Attock. During this onward march the other five rivers of the Panjab were crossed on foot, as they were all fordable in that season. The Chinab was crossed at Wazirabad about 60 m.n.w. of Labor, (8th January 1739).

Zakariya Khan, the governor of Lahor, though unsupported by his master had made what defensive arrangements he could with his own limited resources. Some five thousands of his men, under Qalandar Khan, held the fort of Kacha Mirza † at Yaminabad, 30 miles north of Lahor, as an advanced post, while the governor himself stood with the bulk of his army (probably ten or twelve thousand men) ten miles south, at the Bridge of Shah Daula, The Persian vanguard ** took the fort, killed Qalandar Khan and drove his troops away. At the news of it, Zakariya Khan fell back on Lahor and Nadir advanced to the Bridge of Shah Daula, 20 miles north of that city. From this place, Abdul Baqi Khan, the Persian Wazir, wrote to Zakariya Khan advising him to submit and thus avoid useless bloodshed. [Jahankusha, 343, Hanway, ii. 365-66; Anandram, 16-20.]

† There is a Kot Mirzagan, a little east of Yaminabad, in the Indian Atlas.

** Led by Nasir Kh. acc. to Hanway. Zakariya's total army is put by Ali Hazin at 14 or 15 thousand regular horse and his own militia.

The bank of the Ravi, north of Lahor had been entrenched by Zakariya Khan and big pieces of artillery mounted there to oppose the Persian advance. On 10th January 1739, Nadir marched from the Bridge of Shah Daula, made a wide detour round Lahor, leaving the Mughal defences a long distance on his left, forded the river further downstream and encamped in the Shalimar Garden, five miles east of the city. All that day Zakariya Khan succeeded in repulsing the attempts of the Persians to enter Lahor. The fighting was resumed next day (11th January) but early in the morning the governor's son with a handful of men left the field and made his way to Dihli by long marches. A large force of Indians under the Zamindar of Adina-gar were coming to reinforce Zakariya Khan, when they were overtaken by the Persian skirmishers at Mulkpur, 12 miles from Lahor and dispersed, losing some captives.††

†† The Jahankusha, p 344, is obscure and the lithographed text is corrupt, Adina Beg was Faujdar of Sultanpur, 66 m.s.e. of Lahor, at this time [Tilok Das's poem]. I do not know any Adina-gar. There is a Navowar, 14 m.e. of Lahor but no Mulkpur. Pur may be Haibatpur-Pati. The text of the Jahankusha may also mean that these Indian troops forced their way to Lahor.

Zakariya Khan found resistance vain. No aid could come from Dihli. So, in the afternoon he sent Kifayat Khan, his agent, to Nadir's camp to offer submission and beg for safety. Next day (12th January), he himself went to the victor, delivered the keys of the fort, and presented some large elephants and rare commodities. Nadir treated him kindly but fixed a contribution of 20 lakhs of rupees on the city, part of which was paid out of the Government treasury and the balance assessed on the rich people. On the 14th, the Khan visited the Persian King a second time, paid the money and thus saved the city from the horrors of a sack. * He was received graciously, presented with a robe of honour, an Arab horse with a gold embroidered saddle and costly trappings and jewelled sword and dagger, and retained in the governorship of Lahor. But his second son, Haiyat-ullah Khan, was kept in the Persian king's train at the head of 500 retainers, evidently as a hostage for his father's fidelity.

* Anandram, 23; Jahankusha, 344; Ali Hazin, 293, But Tilok Das says that Lahor was plundered after Nadir's entry into it and that the Persian king, though appealed to, did nothing to restrain his soldiers. At Lahor the invaders first saw the wealth of a large Indian city.

Nadir spent sixteen days at Lahor. Fakhr-ud-daulah, the dismissed governor of Kashmir, who had been living here in great poverty and neglect, was reappointed by Nadir to his post. Nasir Khan was released from captivity and restored to the viceroyalty of Kabul and Peshawar, A Persian force was detached to guard the ferries and seize the boats on the rivers of the Panjab and see that travellers to and from the Persian army during its stay in India could easily pass. Thus, the flanks and rear of the invaders were completely secured.

At Lahor it was definitely learnt that Muhammad Shah had decided on war and was assembling his troops from all sides of his kingdom to oppose the Persians Nadir then wrote a letter to the Emperor, saying that as he was a Turko-man and of the same race as the house of Timur, his intentions were entirely friendly to the Emperor of Dihli, He repeated his former assertion that he had crossed the Mughal frontier solely to punish the Afghans who were as much the enemies of India as of Persia, and he again complained that Muhammad Shah had treated all his three envoys in violation of friendship and diplomatic usage. Lastly, Nadir warned the Mughal Court of the consequences of going to war, though he held forth hopes of his pardon, should the Indian army chiefs, after their defeat, submit to him. [Jahankusha 345-346.]

Nadir's invasion spread ruin and disorder throughout the Panjab. A cavalry screen was by his order sent ahead to make swift raids (turk-tazi) and plunder the cities and richer villages of the province and at the same time reconnoitre the country 30 or 40 miles in advance of his army. At Attack he had instructed his vanguard to plunder and ravage without mercy, "Cities like Wazirabad, Yaminabad, Gujarat, etc, and big villages (each like half a city) were reduced to black ashes. All over the land property was plundered and women outraged," [Anandram, 16 and 21] Tilok Das bears witness to the plunder of Lahore, Jalandhar, and evidently other towns on his route. But this was not the only misery of the province. A foreign invasion gives the wished-for opportunity to the lawless; oppressors and predatory classes, so long controlled by Government, raise their heads when they see the Government engaged in self-defence. Shaikh Ali Haz. who was travelling from Lahor to Sarhind at this time, thus describes the State of things (p. 292); ''The whole province was in complete revolution. Every person put forth his hand to plunder and pillage, and some thousands of robbers beset the public roads.... The whole of that time, whether on the road or at the [halting] stations, passed in fighting and contention."

Nadir Marches from Lahore to Karnal

Leaving Lahore on 26th January 1739, Nadir Shah reached Sarhind on 5th February. Here he learnt that Muhammad Shah was encamped with his army at Karnal, eighty-two miles from him. A force of 6,000 cavalry was sent ahead to reconnoitre the country up to the imperial camp and report on the enemy's strength and dispositions. Next day the main army reached Rajah Sarai [modern Rajpura], 16 miles Southeast of Sarhind and on the day following (7th February) Ambala, 13 miles further east. Here the Persian king left his harem and heavy baggage under a strong escort, while he himself marched out on the 8th with a mobile fighting force and light artillery carried on camels and reached Shahabad, 17 miles east of Ambala, at the end of the day. This place was only 36 miles north of Karnal.

Meantime the Persian scouts had reached the outskirts of the Mughal camp in the night between the 7th and the 8th. They had fallen upon the artillery, killed some men and taken some others captive and finally retired to Sarai Azimabad, *12 miles north of Karnal. The following night these captured Indians were produced before Nadir who questioned them about the Mughal army. The party at Azimabad was strengthened and warned to scout cautiously without precipitating a battle. On the 10th, Nadir resumed his inarch from Shahabad and reached Thanesar (13 m, south) that evening and Sarai Azimabad (10 m. further south) an hour and a half after sunrise on the 11th.

* Azimabad is placed in the map accompanying Thorn's Memoir of the War and also Lett's Atlas about 3 miles north of Taraori and 10 miles south of Thanesar. The Chahar Gulshan gives it as the stage next to Thanesar on the Dihli-Lahore-road (India of Aurangzib).

This Sarai was a big stone and brick house, in which the faujdar and chief men of Ambala had taken refuge. But as soon as the Persian artillery began to play upon it, they cried quarter. Here full information obtained about the imperial encampment at Karnal, which was only twelve miles off. We must now turn to the doings of Muhammad Shah and his advisers.

(Jahankusha, 346-348)

Proceedings of the Imperial Court during Nadir's Invasion

The proceedings of the Dihli Court during Nadir's invasion form a tale of disgraceful inefficiency, amounting to imbecility. The news of the loss of Kabul (19th June 1738) must have reached Dihli in the first week of July, but for several months nothing was done to guard the frontiers. When Nadir crossed the Khaibar Pass (15th Nov), his motive could no longer be mistaken and yet for two months afterwards no energetic step was taken to meet a danger now manifest to all True, on 2nd December 1738, the Emperor had formally given leave to his three highest nobles, Itimad-ud-daulah, Qamar-ud-din Khan (the wazir), Nizam-ul-mulk Asaf Jah (the Wakil or Regent) and Samsam-ud-daulah Khan Dauran (the Amir-ul-umara and Bakhshi or the head of the military department), to set out against the invader and one kror of rupees had been granted to them for their expenses. They encamped outside Dihli in the Shalimar garden near Sarai Baoli and wasted full one month there.*

The news of Nadir Shah having crossed the river at Attock must have reached Dihli on 10th January 1739. Then the imperial army was urged to hurry on. The Court still hoped for much from the stand to be made by Zakariya Khan whom they had refused to reinforce. But when that poor governor proved no match for the world-conqueror, the cry of treachery was raised; the Hindustani party at Court falsely accused the Khan of having disloyally surrendered Lahore fort to the Persians, as he was a man from Khurasan like Nadir himself.

[Shakir]

At the first bruit of Nadir Shah's invasion, the imperial Court had discovered its incompetence and summoned the Nizam to give it counsel. He was the last survivor of the great age of Aurangzeb, a grey-haired veteran of many fights, a man rich in the experience of life and an expert in diplomacy. But the Nizam was not given the supreme command and dictatorial authority which such a crisis required, nor did he enjoy the confidence of his master whose ears were possessed by Khan Dauran and the Hindustani party. This Khan Dauran had a very high opinion of Rajput valour. He caused farmans to be sent summoning to the emperor's aid his own proteges, the Hindu Rajah's, especially Sawai Jai Singh. But Rajputana had been hopelessly alienated since Aurangzeb's time and Jai Singh and other chieftains were now aiming at political salvation by declaring their independence and calling in the Mahrattas to help in dissolving the Empire. The Rajahs made excuses and delayed coming. Muhammad Shah even appealed to Baji Rao, as we learn from the following letter of the Peshwa to his general Pilaji Jadon:

* Hanway (ii 360) says that Khan Dauran stopped here owing to the Nizam's jealousy and discord. The Dihli Chronicle says that accountants for their armies were appointed as late as 14th and 20th December, —they took things so leisurely. No doubt, this month (2, 31 Dec.) was Ramzan or the month of fasting. But Aurangzeb had campaigned in Ramzan.

"I shall march to Northern India by regular stages. The Persian sovereign Tahmasp Quli has come to conquer the world. To help Muhammad Shah, I am sending the Malwa force under Malhar Rao Holkar, Ranuji Sindhia, and [Udaji] Puar. It is a glory to this monarchy [i.e., the Mahratta State] to help the Emperor of Dihli at such a time." [Raj. vi, No. 130] But reliance on the Mahrattas, even if seriously contemplated, proved like leaning on a broken reed. No Dakhini force came to the emperor's assistance at Karnal or even in time to defend Dihli after the imperial defeat in the field. On the contrary, the Mahratta enjoy in the emperor's camp at Karnal was glad to make his escape by jungle paths on 25th February and seek safety by retreating as far south as Jaipur, Baji Rao himself in his next letter is found contemplating the defence of the Narmada line to bar the southward advance of Nadir. A Mahratta defence of Northern India was not to be thought of.

The imperial forces passed the month of Ramzan [December 1738] outside Dihli in utter idleness. Then came the news of the Persians having crossed at Attock. So, at last on 10th January 1739, the three nobles began to march towards Lahore, after urging the emperor with one breath and extreme emphasis that he should join the army in person. On the 18th they reached Panipat, 55 miles north of Dihli.

On that day (18th January), Muhammad Shah himself issued from Dihli and on the 27th he reached Panipat, where his generals had been halting for nine days in expectation of his coming! Nadir's capture of Lahore had already been learnt by the Court and it was found too late to save that city. So, it was decided to encamp and wait for the enemy at Karnal, where there was an abundance of water from Ali Mardan's canal, and the extensive plain around supplied opportunities for manoeuvring large bodies of cavalry. A halt was also necessary to enable Saadat Khan, the governor of Oudh, to join with his 30,000 horsemen. Reinforcements were also expected from Rajputana.

The emperor's advisers, particularly the Nizam, therefore, decided to entrench at Karnal instead of risking a battle. Under the direction of Sad-ud-din Khan, Mir Atash, the camp was enclosed with a mud-wall many miles in circuit. Along this line the guns were ranged side by side; soldiers were posted in the trenches to keep watch day and night. [Anandram. 25; Shakir 40; Chronicle; Siyar, i. 96: Bayan 32, Jauhar-i-samsam in Elliot viii, 74.]

The Rival forces at Karnal: the imperial encampment

The Persian army at Karnal is estimated by Rustam Ali at 55,000 horses. This number is nearest the truth. We know from Mirza Mahdi's history that Nadir Shah had started from Persia with 80,000 troops and though he had enlisted Afghans on the way and possibly also received drafts from home, he had to detach large forces to garrison the many conquered forts and guard the long line of communication in his rear, as well as to escort his eldest son on his return to Persia. Hanway says that Nadir reached Tilawri (i. e., Taraori near Azimabad) with 40,000 men; this was clearly exclusive of his vanguard and rear. The entire Persian camp contained 160,000 souls of whom one-third were servants, but these were all mounted and some of them completely armed, so that they could take part in plunder and the defence of their baggage. There were also more than 6,000 women, dressed in great coats (barani) of crimson cloth, like the men and not to be distinguished from the latter at a distance, [Hanway, ii, 367.]

The imperial army is put by Nadir's secretary at three hundred thousand renowned soldiers',*2,000 fighting elephants and 3,000 pieces of artillery. Rustam All's figures are two hundred thousand horse, innumerable foot, 1,500 elephants and many guns, [Elliot, viii, 60,] The numbers are still further exaggerated by the later Lakhnau historian Ghulam Ali, who gives five hundred thousand horse and foot, 8,000 pieces of artillery of all calibres and 11,000 tents, [Imad, 24.] Anandram who was a secretary to the Wazir and accompanied the army to Panipat puts the number as 50,000 horsemen besides the personal contingents of the three nobles. We know that the Nizam had brought with himself only 3,000 men. So, the total Indian fighting force at Karnal could not have exceeded 75,000 men.

* So many could not have been all renowned! Hanway gives "nearly two hundred thousand, the great part of which was cavalry,"

But the number of non-combatants with it was excessive. Even at the end of the 18th century a modern European army operating in the same area carried nine non-combatants to one fighter. Lord Lake's camp contained three hundred thousand souls, out of whom only 30,000 were soldiers. As the Emperor himself with his harem and the luxurious grandees with their families were present, we shall not be wrong in estimating the population in the camp at Karnal at a million men.

The circuit of the Indian camp is said by one authority to have been twelve miles. [Hanway, ii, 364] But such an enormous length of wall could not be adequately defended against an active enemy with a very mobile cavalry and light artillery carried on camels. The result was that the Indian army from the very outset lost its mobility and aggressive power and became helplessly beleaguered like the Mahratta army of Sadashiv Bhao in the town of Panipat 22 years later.

The wrong strategy of the emperor became evident as soon as the enemy came into touch and made the neighbourhood unsafe for small parties. The Indian army, owing to its vast number, —a million souls, besides animals, —could scarcely find space to encamp on. The Persian horsemen made attack from all sides, and carried off corn, grass, and fuel, so that the price of grain rose enormously in the camp, * [Rustam Ali.] Within four days of the battle of Karnal this huge mass of men had eaten up all their store of food and then after five days of fasting the entire army surrendered.

* Ali Hazin, then at Dihli, says the same thing: "The Indians, having gathered their artillery around, were closely hemmed in by their own fieldpieces and as a division of the Qizilbashes had also formed a ring on every side of them, all intercourse with the outside was closed to them and dearth and famine fell on that army Muhammad Shah, and his innumerable multitude, finding the Qizilbash cavalry spread around them on all sides, were afraid to stir and although they saw themselves unable to maintain their position, they remained on the spot."

Nadir comes into touch with Indian army at Karnal, 12th February.

The city of Karnal lies on the ancient highway from Dihli to Lahore, about 75 miles north of the Mughal capital, 20 miles north of Panipat, and nine miles south of Taraori, where so many historic battles for deciding the lordship of Northern India have been fought. Even Kurukshetra, the scene of the mythical warfare between the Panduvas and Kauravas is only 22 miles north of it. Hence it was in the natural fitness of things that the decisive encounter between India and Persia took place at Karnal.

The canal of Ali Mardan Khan skirts the eastern side of the town. Between this canal and the river Jamuna east of it, there is a plain five to seven miles in breadth, fit for cavalry manoeuvres on a large scale. Muhammad Shah had formed his entrenched camp along the western bank of the canal, with the walled town of Karnal immediately south of him. Sarai Azimabad, the last station of the invaders, stands 12 miles north of Karnal and some ten miles west of the canal. The first eight miles of the ground between Azimabad and Karnal were then covered with a dense jungle * with a single narrow path crossing it. The four miles immediately north of Karnal were a level plain free from jungles. Muhammad Shah's front and right were, therefore, naturally protected by the jungle and the canal, respectively. The disposition of the Indian army was the Nizam in the van facing the north or slightly northwest with artillery on two sides of him, the Wazir in the left or west, the emperor in the centre and Khan Dauran in the right or east. [Jahankusha 346, 348; Hanway, ii, 364.]

* This jungle continued till the early years of the 19th century. Thorn (Memoir of the war, P. 480) writes in 1805 about the tract from Dihli to Sonepat, "The whole of this country which was formerly fertilized by a canal dug by Ali Mardan Khan, is now overgrown with jungle and is generally in a very desolate state."

Nadir Shah had arrived at Sarai Azimabad early in the morning of Sunday, 11th February 1739. A force of 6,000 horsemen, composed of the best troops of Kurdistan, led by Haji Khan, divided into two bodies, had previously reconnoitred the country along both banks of the canal up to the very edge of the imperial camp. These scouts now reported on the state of the ground and produced prisoners captured outside the Mughal lines.

Learning the exact dispositions of the imperial army and the condition of the ground in its environs. Nadir Shah decided to avoid a frontal attack and make a wide detour along the east of Karnal, so as to keep touch with the Jamuna and its abundant water supply on his left flank and also to cut Mughal line of communication with Dihli by seizing the town of Panipat in the rear. His strategy was intended to force Muhammad Shah to come out of his lines and accept battle on a field chosen by Nadir or to remain helplessly shut up in Karnal while the Persians would march to Dihli unmolested. [Jahankusha, 348.] This plan succeeded admirably and much sooner than was expected.

Before sunrise on Monday, 12th February, the Persian army marched out of Sarai Azimabad, crossed the canal some nine miles east of that town, and encamped on a level plain six miles north-east of Karnal, evidently a little north of Kunjpura and within sight of the Jamuna. While the main division halted here, Nadir with a small escort galloped to the neighbourhood of Muhammad Shah's position which was indicated by his standards and flags and the concentration of artillery round it. After reconnoitring the enemy's numbers and dispositions, he returned to his own tents.

In the evening a report was brought to him that Saadat Khan, who was coming from Oudh to the aid of the emperor with 30,000 cavalries, artillery and stores had reached Panipat. Immediately a division of the Persian army was told off to intercept him. A second and very strong division was detached that very night to threaten the eastern flank of the Mughal camp, though small bodies of skirmishers had been already hovering round it at a mile's distance, cutting off stragglers. [Jahankusha, 349.]

Karnal: Indians Issue for combat

The fatal Tuesday, the 13th of February 1739, dawned. The Persian army advanced from its position in three divisions along the plain between the canal and the Jamuna, a belt nearly five miles in breadth. Prince Nasr-ullah, in charge of the Centre, was ordered to march from the bank of the Jamuna* and take post north of Muhammad Shah's camp, facing the Nizam's division. Nadir Shah himself, at the head of the vanguard, first arrived opposite the Indian position on the canal, but learning on the way that Saadat Khan had joined the emperor at midnight, he swerved aside to his left and pitched his camp on a spacious field, three miles east of the enemy and a mile or two west of the Jamuna. Here his son joined him with the Centre. In these movements the forenoon was passed, and the sun had begun to decline from the meridian when suddenly the Indians were seen coming out of their lines to offer battle.

* Mirza Mahdi says, 'from the northern side of the river Jamuna,' which implies that the prince's division had been thrown across the rivers the day before, in order to protect Nadir's left flank. Not likely.

To understand how this happened, it is necessary for us to know the events in the imperial camp. On receiving his master's appeal for aid, Saadat Khan had left his province of Oudh at the head of 20,000 horse, artillery, and materials of war and made successive marches for one month to reach Kamal. He had arrived at Dihli on 7th February and halted there for one day only. The 55 miles between Dihli and Panipat were covered in three days and then on the 4th day, the 12th of February, he made a supreme effort and passed the remaining 20 miles, reaching Karnal at midnight with the main part of his army, while his camp and baggage slowly straggled behind, in a long line insufficiently guarded, one day's march behind, as was the usual thing with Indian armies.

We have seen that on the 12th the Persian scouts had advanced 32 miles from their own camp and secured news of Saadat Khan's position at Panipat. But the intelligence department of the Indian army seems to have been hopelessly careless or inefficient. Saadat Khan had not found out the enemy's whereabouts, nor taken care to protect his baggage train against a possible attack. The emperor himself at Karnal had been equally careless. As Ghulam Husain writes, "None in the imperial camp knew of the near arrival of Nadir from Lahore, till one day some men of the corn-dealers (banjaras) who had gone six or eight miles outside to bring in fodder, came back wounded and panic-stricken after a sudden encounter with the Persian scouts and the cry ran through the encampment 'Nadir has come! Nadir has come!' A mortal fear seized the army and the longing for Saadat Khan's arrival became keener." [i, 96.]

About midnight, 12th February, Saadat Khan arrived near Karnal. He was welcomed a mile in advance by Khan Dauran and conducted within the lines. In the morning, he waited on the emperor. After the usual courtesies had been exchanged, a council of war was held in the imperial presence and plans of operations were being discussed, when news arrived that the Persian advanced skirmishers had fallen upon Saadat Khan's baggage and were carrying off 500 loaded camels. [Harcharan.]

The Khan immediately took up his sword which he had laid down on the carpet before the emperor and asked for permission to depart and fight the Persians*. The Nizam counselled delay, urging that the Oudh soldiers were worn out by one month's incessant marching and required some days' rest to become fit again. Moreover, the sun had already begun to decline, and they would have only three hours of daylight left for fighting after reaching the field. Khan Dauran also pointed out that as the imperial troops had not been previously warned to be ready to fight that day, they would take a long time to assemble arm and form line of battle. It was (The two-nobles urged) therefore better to fight the next day, when they would be able to advance in proper array with artillery and full preparations and to follow their accustomed tactics. One courtier even told Saadat Khan that 500 camels were nothing to a man like him and that if he could defeat Nadir Shah, —as they hoped to do easily by a pitched battle the next day, — the entire Persian royal camp and its wealth would be their prey.

But he would not listen to this advice and insisted on going out to the rescue of his camp followers. Sending out some heralds to proclaim in his camp that all his soldiers should assemble and follow him, he hastened to the point of attack with only his escort and the troops within call, amounting to a thousand horse and a few hundred feet but without any artillery. The Indian cavalryman's employment depended upon the life of his horse, which was his own property and therefore he was most reluctant to risk it or fatigue it too much. After a month of fast riding, they refused to stir out that day, saying that as their master had gone to visit the emperor he could not possibly have issued for battle. Still, nearly 4,000 cavalry and 1,000 infantries joined him in the end. [Bayan, 34; Anandram, 27.]

---

*Harcharan says that the emperor distrusted Saadat Khan for being a native of Persia and made him swear fidelity on the Quran in his presence. Siyar asserts that Saadat had taken leave of the emperor and was waiting for his baggage in the quarters assigned to him (behind those of Khan Dauran) when he learnt of the attack. But Shakir Kh. (then in the camp) Abdul Karim and Harcharan say that he heard the report in the emperor's darbar. The Dihii Chronicle says that the emperor ordered Saadat to go out and attack the Persians, Anandram says that the emperor overruled Khan Dauran's objection to fighting on that day. All other authorities hold that the emperor agreed with the Nizam to defer the action till next day.

As Saadat Khan came to the field, the Persian skirmishers pretended flight; he gave them chase and was thus lured away to a distance of two miles from his camp. He sent off couriers to the emperor begging for reinforcements to complete the victory. Muhammad Shah took counsel of the Nizam, who replied that as the fight was in the east of imperial camp, Khan Dauran who commanded the division nearest to that point viz., the Right Wing, should go. Khan Dauran obeyed the order * and issued forth on an elephant without waiting to assemble his full contingent or drag out his artillery. As he was very popular with the soldiers, many of them, on hearing of his having issued to battle, armed, and joined him of their own accord in successive drafts, till at last he had some 8,000 horses round him.

---

*Immediately (according to Bayan) or after some grumbling, according to Anandram.

Later, in the afternoon, the emperor himself marched out of his tents with the Wazir and stood with marshalled ranks by the side of the canal, but more as a distant spectator of the battle than as a participator in it. The delay in the starting of the different divisions, the absence of a common pre-arranged plan of battle and the lack of one supreme director of operations on the Indian side, led to their three divisions being separated from one another by more than a mile's interval, Saadat Khan formed the Right Wing which was in the extreme east and near the Jumuna, Khan Dauran's division now became the Centre and stood in the middle of the plain, while the Wazir and the Emperor formed the Left Wing bordering on the canal. Gradually, by the end of the day, when the successive groups of imperialists had marched up to the field, they formed a vast concourse of men, filling the wide plain from their own camp to the place of conflict, with two intervals as described above. The Left Wing (under the emperor) had dragged out field artillery from behind the shelter of the trenches and had also pitched small tents in the plain for its chiefs; it did not, however, engage the enemy at all.

But this army was a mob, it lacked cohesion; it had no animating soul, no unity of command nor indeed any leading at all. The main portion of it stood stock-still, far away from the point of impact, without contributing anything to the struggle and their vast number only caused a vaster butchery during the retreat. The extremely mobile enemy, led by the greatest living general in Asia, struck the Indian host or evaded it as they found most advantageous to them. Nadir Shah's genius neutralized the superiority in numbers and the desperate valour of many of the Indian soldiers.

Battle of Karnal 13th February

When, a little after midday, Saadat Khan's army was seen to come forth to the plain, news of it was at once carried to Nadir. He was highly elated to hear of it. He had been wishing for such a day, as, his Court historian remarks, and it had come unexpectedly soon. The Indian army had been drawn out of its strongly entrenched position and at last a battle of manoeuvres was possible in which the Persian general could show his genius.

Nadir's arrangements were swiftly made, so as not to let the enemy escape through nightfall before his work of destruction was fully done. He left a division to guard his camp; his Centre was placed in charge of his son Nasr-ullah with many noted warriors and a powerful artillery. The vanguard was under his own command. Three thousand of his best troops were formed into three different bodies and placed in ambush. Two small bodies, each consisting of 500 swift horsemen, were sent against Saadat Khan and Khan Dauran in order to draw them further into the field.* Nadir himself, clad in full armour and wearing an ornamented helmet, mounted a fleet horse and marched into the fight with one thousand picked Turkish horsemen of his own clan (the Afshar), to direct the battle. The Persian army was entirely composed of cavalry and their artillery consisted of Jazair, i.e., long muskets or swivel-guns, seven or eight feet in length, with a prong to rest on. In addition, there were zamburaas or long swivels firing one-or two-pound balls; "each of these pieces, with its stock, was mounted on a camel, which lay down at command and 'from the backs of these animals, trained to this exercise, they charged and fired these guns." [Jahankusha, 351; Hanway, ii, 368, 153.]

* Bayan differs: "Nadir's Right Wing was placed under Tahmasp Quli Jalair, left under Path Ali and Luft Ali Afshar, Centre under Nasr-ullah and the vanguard, consisting of 4,000 cavalries carrying jazair, under himself."

In order to baffle the elephants, on which the Indians mostly relied for effect, he caused a number of platforms to be made and fixed each across two camels. On these platforms he laid naphtha and a mixture of combustibles with orders to set them on fire during the battle. The elephants were sure to flee away at the sight of the quickly approaching fire and put the Indian army behind them in disorder.

[Hanway, ii., 369.]

The Persian skirmishers had effectively screened their main position where Nadir had stationed 3,000 of his best troops, dismounted his swivels and ranged them along the front with their barrels resting on prongs.

The battle began a little after one o'clock in the afternoon with a discharge of arrows on both sides. The Persian scouts pretended flight, turning back in their saddle, and discharging their bows and muskets while galloping, in the manner of their Parthian ancestors. Saadat Khan gave chase and was thus drawn to the ambush three or four miles east of the imperial camp and the support of its artillery. Suddenly the cavalry screen drew aside in front and Saadat Khan's army was assailed by the discharge of many hundred swivel-guns at point-blank range. [Harcharan.] The bravest of his troopers who rode foremost fell. After standing this murderous fire for a short while, the Indian vanguard fled. [Anandram.] But Saadat Khan maintained his ground for some time longer, amidst a band of devoted followers, who fought to the death. But early in the evening he was forced out of the field, and the fight in the extreme Right of the Mughal army ceased.

The same fate overtook Khan Dauran's division in another part of the field (the Centre), though he made a longer stand. The rapid fire of the Persian swivel-guns carried death into his ranks, without a chance of reply.

The masterly tactics of Nadir, aided by the recklessness and utter want of generalship of the Indian chiefs, had separated the three divisions of the imperial army from one another by more than a mile's interval, so that the soldiers of each division merely heard the sound of firing in the other parts of the field, but could learn nothing of the plight of their brethren, much less hasten to their aid. Khan Dauran could not co-operate with his friend Saadat Khan, however much he wished it. The Nizam, though the ablest general on the Indian side, was absolutely inert throughout the day and gave no help to Khan Dauran or Saadat Khan, probably because he hoped (as Abdul Karim suggests) to take the places of these rivals at Court if they perished. The emperor was imbecile and stood like a wooden figure in the extreme Left. At the points of contact the Indians had a numerical inferiority and were far away from the aid of their heavy artillery. Their generals mounted on tall elephants became targets for the enemy's fire, while the nimble Persian horsemen hovered round beyond the reach of the weapons of the Indians.

The murderous fire of Nadir's gunners continued for two hours. The Indians fought bravely but gave up their lives as a vain sacrifice because (in the words of Abdul Karim) "arrows cannot answer bullets." When the situation became absolutely hopeless and most of their officers had fallen, about 1,000 of the bravest soldiers of Khan Dauran dismounted and, in the Indian fashion, tying the skirts of their long coats together, fought on foot till they all died. [Bayan.] Khan Dauran himself had been mortally wounded in the face and fallen down unconscious on his howda. But a party of devoted retainers, under his steward Majlis Rai, surrounded his elephant and by desperate fighting brought him back to the camp, near sunset, but only to die. [Anandram.]

Defeat and casualties of the Indians.

Saadat Khan had been suffering for the last three months from a wound in the leg which prevented him from riding or walking and he used to be carried about in a chair or on an elephant. Though he had received two wounds in this battle, he could have retired in safety but for an accident. His elephant was charged by the infuriated elephant of his nephew Nisar Muhammad Khan Sher Jang and driven into the Persian 'ranks, though his men stabbed it with sword and dagger to make it stop. Surrounded by enemies, Saadat Khan continued to shoot arrows from his seat, to resist capture, when a young Persian soldier of his native city of Naishabur boldly galloped up to his elephant and addressing him by his familiar name, cried out, "Muhammad Amin! Are you mad? Whom are you fighting? On whom are you still relying?" Then driving his spear into the ground and throwing the reins of his horse round it, he climbed up to Saadat Khan's howda by the rope hanging down from it. The Khan now surrendered and was taken to Nadir's camp. [Siyar, i, 97.]

At the disappearance of these two leaders, the Indian army melted away, pursued by the Persian horsemen with heavy slaughter. The emperor with his other nobles stood in battle order by the side of the canal (in the extreme west of the field) expecting an attack. But Nadir Shah kept his men back from assaulting such a strongly fortified position and its heavy artillery; he had a surer and easier means of compelling the emperor's submission. At sunset, Muhammad Shah retired to his camp, after having all that day done absolutely nothing to save his throne and his people.* The battle was over in less than three hours; it had commenced at the time of the zuhar prayer and ended at the asar prayer. [Jahankusha, 351.]

* I reject the absurd story told in Bayan, p. 41. Hanway (ii, 369) says that in the night following the battle the Indian camp was so very thin that from the emperor's own quarters to those of the Nizam, which was nearly two miles off, hardly any people were found.

The slaughter in the Indian army was terrible. Nadir's court historian gives the exaggerated figures of 100 chiefs and 30,000 common soldiers slain and a vast number taken prisoner. [Jahankusha 353.] Hanway shortly afterwards heard in Persia of 17,000 Indians having been killed. Harcharandas gives 20,000 and the Mahratta envoy in the imperial camp 10 to 12 thousand men in one account and seven to eight thousand in a later report. [Brahmendra S C., No. 41] Rustam Ali says that Khan Dauran alone lost 5,000 men, to which we must add at least 3,000 for Saadat Khan's division, making a total of 8,000 slain.

Among the officers slain were Muzaffar Khan (a younger brother of Khan Dauran), three sons of Khan Dauran (Ali Hamid, Muhataram and another), Aslih Khan (the commander of the Emperor's bodyguard), Ali Ahmad Khan," Shahdad Afghan, Yadgar Hasan Khan (Koka), Ashraf Khan, Itibar Khan, Aqil Beg Kambalposh ('Blanket-wearer'), Mir Kalu (son of Mir Mushrif) and Ratan chand (son of the historian Khushhal chand, who was office-assistant to the imperial paymaster). Saadat Khan and his nephew Sher Jang, as well as Khwaja Ashura (a son of Khan Dauran) were captured alive.

The loss on the Persian side was 2,500 slain and twice as many wounded, according to Hanway, who estimates the Indian casualties in slain as seven times the number of the Persians killed. This relative proportion seems to me to be nearest the truth, though the figures for both sides are exaggerated.*

* The bed-ridden invalid Ali Hazin, who is eternally cursing India, its climate, and people, says that the Persians lost only 3 killed and 20 wounded 1 Siyar and Ghulam Ali blindly copy these figures.

The gains of the Victor were immense. Of the elephants, field treasury, guns, baggage, and stores of all kinds taken outside the entrenchment, nothing escaped. The booty was beyond count. As soon as Saadat Khan and Khan Dauran were seen to leave the field, their camps were plundered by their own followers and the miscellaneous rabble that accompanied Mughal armies. In a twinkle no trace of these two nobles' vast encampments, not even a tent, was left on their sites. [Shakir, Siyar i. 96.] When the half-dead body of Khan Dauran was brought back, his servants had to borrow a small poleless tent from elsewhere to shelter his head in.

A great terror befell the Indian army. All night long the remaining soldiers stood on guard along the camp enclosure, armed and with their horses saddled, ready to meet the enemy's attack. [Shakir; Chronicle.]

Causes of the Indian defeat at Karnal

The defeat of the Indians at Karnal was due as much to their being outclassed in their weapons of war and method of fighting, as to their bad generalship.

Nadir was not really a Persian, but a Turk of a tribe settled on the Persian soil for centuries past. His soldiers were Turks and other nomads (like the Kurds), and not Persians proper. He conversed with Muhammad Shah in Turkish. [Harcharan.] Indeed, the Persians themselves designated his army accurately by calling them Qizil-bashes or Red Caps, from the scarlet broad-cloth caps worn by them, —the very caps which we see today on the heads of the Turks and their imitators in Egypt and India. The true Persians are an Aryan people, with a strong Semitic strain infused into them after the Muslim conquest but they have little Turanian or Turkish racial admixture. Their language is not akin to Turkish, their manners are different from those of the Turks and their religion is the opposite of that Sunnism of which Turkey and the Turks are the orthodox champions. The Persians proper (the same race as the Parsis now settled in India) are very intelligent, refined, proud, and possessed of a delicate sense of humour, but no soldiers. Nadir's troops, the Qizil-bashes, were men of the same race and same method of warfare as the so-called Pathan and Mughal conquerors of India, namely Turks and Turkomans from Central Asia, capable of making long and rapid rides and bearing every privation on the way.

In addition to this, Nadir's army contained a large proportion of men equipped with firearms, several thousands of jazair-chis, or swivel-gunners. Their discipline was strict, and their fire control was of the European type. They used to reserve their fire till the word of command and then deliver a volley. The effect on their enemy was as disconcerting as it was deadly. At Karnal, the Persian swivel-guns were planted in rows on the ground and kept ready for the Indians, who were lured there by the skirmishers and then their rapid fire completely overthrew the enemy without giving them a chance to retaliate.

---

* "The battlefield became a bed of poppies from the crowd of Qizilbash troops, all of whom wore Turk-like [?] caps of red sqarlat." [Anandram, 29.]

The Indian cavalry prided itself on its swordsmanship and cultivated swordplay and fancy riding, as if war were a theatrical show. They fought with the sword only and felt a contempt for missile weapons and those who used them. In describing the battles with the Persians for the possession of Qandahar in the middle of the 17th century, the Dihli Court historian sneers at the Persian troopers for declining sword combats with the cavaliers of Hindustan. He taunts the Persians with cowardice pretty nearly in the same tone as the English writers employed during the last war in speaking of the German soldiers, who did not stand up-to receive the bayonet charges of the British infantry.

The Indian Musalman and Rajput soldiers were very inefficient in the use of firearms. The only musketeers of any value in the Mughal army in the 17th century were the Hindus of Buxar, the Bundelas, the Karnatakis (of whom there were many in the service of the Bijapur Sultans but none under the Later Mughals), and a small class of hunters called Bachelias usually recruited in the Allahabad province. The immense majority of the Indian soldiers did not fight with muskets, nor did they, as a rule, carry into the field portable light artillery of the jazair class in large numbers. The Indian ordnances were heavy, cumbrous and of a more antiquated type than those of Persia and Turkey, and therefore the fire delivered by them was usually slow and inaccurate enough to be neglected. The Indian soldiers were trained to stake everything on the shock charge of heavy cavalry and hand to hand grapple. They had little mobility. Not so the Qizilbashes in the Persian service. Like their fellow Turanians in Trans-oxiana or in the armies of the Usmanli Sultans of Constantinople, they formed the best cavalry in Asia, —hardy and fast horsemen, mounted on fleetest and strongest breed of horses and trained to the saddle from their childhood, as became a normal race. They were also capital archers, accustomed to shoot from the saddle and fight while fleeing. They had a decisive advantage over the Indians, as men fighting with missiles have over those who can employ side-arms only.

The superior mobility of Nadir's soldiers enabled them to assume the offensive from the very beginning. They outmanoeuvred the Indians and drove them to the place most advantageous to the attacking party; they fought or deferred engagement as it suited them.

The Indian's crowning folly was the employment of elephants in this modern age of muskets and comparatively long-range artillery carried on camels. Elephants had failed against mobile cavalry using missiles in the almost pre-historic times of Alexander the Great when firearms were unknown and more recently against Babar's horsemen with their few slow and primitive guns. They were a sure engine of self-destruction when ranged against Nadir Shah in the year 1739.

Negotiations for peace with Nadir Shah

When Nadir Shah returned to his camp from the battlefield Saadat Khan was brought before him, after the isha prayer (8 p. m.). The king spoke contemptuously of the Indian army as a 'host of beggars' and remarked of their general Khan Dauran that he knew how to die but not how to fight. [Imad,] He then inquired about the resources and intentions of the emperor. Saadat Khan diplomatically replied: "The Emperor's resources are vast. Only one of his nobles came out to "fight today and has gone back on being accidentally wounded by a shot. But there are many other amirs and brave Rajahs with countless hosts still left." Nadir Shah remarked; "You are my fellow-countryman and fellow-believer. Advise me how I can get a ransom from your Emperor and go home to fight the Sultan of Turkey." Saadat Khan then advised him to summon the Nizam who was "the Key of the Stale of India" and settle peace terms through him."* Next day, 14th February, Nadir Shah sent a man with the Quran io Muhammad Shah to lake an oath on it as to his good Faith and call the Nizam. Saadat Khan also wrote to the emperor, advising him to send the Nizam and make peace.

---

* This history of the negotiations is mainly based upon Harcharandas (who is supported by Rustam Ali, Elliot, viii, 62) with some useful points from the Chronicle, Mahratti letters, Anandram 33-36; Jahankusha, 354; Siyar 97-98; Bayan, 43-44.

The Nizam was now the last of the great nobles at the side of the emperor, and the latter was naturally alarmed at the thought of sending him away. He asked, "If any treachery is done to you, what steps should we take?" The Nizam replied, "The Quran is between us. If there is treachery, God will answer for it. Then your Majesty should retreat to Mandu or some other strong fort, summon Nasir Jang from the Dakhin with a strong force and fight the Persian."

The Nizam then left for the Persian camp with full powers to negotiate. Nadir received him well and complained, "It is surprising that while there are nobles like you on the emperor's side, the naked Mahrattas can march up to the walls of Dihii and take ransom from him!" The Nizam replied, "Since new nobles rose to influence, his Majesty did whatever he liked. My advice was not acceptable to him. Therefore, in helplessness I left him and retired to the Dakhin."

The reply pleased Nadir. Turning to the subject of peace, he complained of the unfriendly indifference of the Dihli Government during his struggles with his enemies, though the former sovereigns of Persia had often helped the emperor's forefathers. The Nizam explained it by saying "Since the death of Farrukhsiyar, the affairs of this Government have gone to rack and ruin owing to quarrels among the nobles and therefore the ministers did not attend to your Majesty's letters."

After a long discussion, it was agreed that the Persian army would go back from that place on being promised a war indemnity of 50 lakhs* of rupees, out of which 20 lakhs were to be paid then and there, 10 lakhs on reaching Lahore, ten lakhs at Attock, and the remaining ten lakhs at Kabul. After making this settlement the Nizam took his leave. Nadir sent with him an invitation to the emperor to dine with him the next day.

On Thursday, 15th February† Muhammad Shah accompanied by all his nobles started for the Persian camp, the Nizam instructing him that he would have to converse with Nadir in the Turkish language. The Persian Wazir met the party on the way and vowed on the Quran that no treachery would be done to them. Outside the Persian encampment Prince Nasrullah welcomed the guest on behalf of his father. On their arrival, Nadir advanced to outside his tent, took Muhammad Shah graciously by the hand and leading him within, seated him on the royal carpet by his own side. The Nizam, the Wazir and Muhammad Ishaq Khan were permitted to go inside, all others remained outside the tent.

---

* The Siyar (97) puts the figure at 2 krors. Not true.

† The Dihli Chronicle gives the date as 18th February, which is contradicted by Mahdi, Harcharan, and all other authorities.

As the two sovereigns were talking together, Ishaq Khan (Muta-man-ud-daulah) joined in the conversation. Nadir Shah in anger asked who the man was that had ventured to mingle his speech with that of kings. Muhammad Shah then introduced him as the tutor (ataliq) of his childhood. The Persian king put questions to Ishaq Khan and was so much pleased with his ready and intelligent answers that he pronounced him fit to be the Wazir of India. [Harcharan.]

The party then sat down to dinner. The Persian conqueror proudly remarked, "My practice is open war and not treacherous assassination" and then, in order to assure Muhammad Shah that his food was not poisoned, he exchanged his own dishes with those of the emperor just as they were about to begin eating. [Harcharan.] As an act of courtesy, Nadir Shah himself handed the cup of coffee to the emperor. The meeting ended happily and about three hours before sunset Muhammad Shah took leave of his host and returned to his own camp. Here his family and servants and indeed the whole camp had been passing the hours of his absence in the greatest fear and anxiety expecting his murder or at least captivity at the hands of Nadir. His safe return now, in the words of the historian, "restored to them the hearts which had left their bodies." [Anandram; Bayan,] But the Persian investment of the Indian camp continued. [Jahan.]

Samsam-ud-daulah Khan Dauran, the head of the army (Amir-ul-umara and Bakhshi-ul-mamalik) died on the 15th. The story goes that when in the evening of the fatal 13th of February his senseless body was brought back to the site of his plundered camp, the Nizam, the Wazir, and the emperor's eunuchs came to inquire after his condition and offer condolences and prayers. Khan Dauran came to his senses for a while, opened his eyes and whispered in a very weak voice, "I have myself finished my own business. Now you know and your work knows. Never take the Emperor to Nadir, nor conduct Nadir to Dihli, but send away that evil from this point by any means that you can devise," [Siyar.] He then relapsed into unconsciousness and died after less than two days.*

---

*Anandram definitely asserts that he survived only one day after the battle. Mirza Mahdi says (P.352) that he died the day after the battle and M.U. (i. 819) supports this. Ghulam Ali (P. 25) makes him linger not more than one night. The Mahratta envoy's letter places his death 2 or 3 days after the battle, Harcharandas makes the emperor learn of his death four gharis after nightfall on the 15th. Bayan has the 3rd day after the battle. The Dihli Chronicle, however, gives 17th February as the date of his death and the Siyar repeats it.

The emperor on returning from his first visit to Nadir Shah, heard of the death of Khan Dauran. The Nizam immediately afterwards came to him and induced him to confer the deceased noble's office of Paymaster on his own son Firuz Jang, as a reward for his diplomatic success in turning Nadir Shah back. [Siyar.] At this, Azim-ullah Khan, the son of the Wazir's brother, was filled with despair and envy and immediately started for the Persian camp with his own retainers to join Nadir, saying, "I am older than Firuz Jang. Why has the Bakhshi's post been conferred on Firuz Jang, while 1 am available?"

The Nizam and the Wazir hastened after him and brought him back from the way. As the Nizam was older than Azim-ullah, he assumed the office of Bakhshi himself and thus Azim-ullah was silenced. A truce was thus patched up at Court. But when Saadat Khan in the Persian camp heard of the Nizam's appointment as Bakhshi, the fire of his jealousy blazed forth, as he had long coveted this post and the Nizam had promised to help him in getting it. He now set to wreak vengeance on his successful rival and his ungrateful master. At his next audience with Nadir Shah, Saadat Khan told him how unwise he was in being satisfied with an indemnity of 50 lakhs because if the conqueror went to Dihli 20 krors in cash and jewels and other valuable articles beyond estimate would be easily secured. "At present," Saadat Khan pointed out, "The imperial Court has no noble of eminence except the Nizam, who is a cheat and a philosopher. If this deceiver is entrapped, everything would happen as your Majesty desired. If you order me, I shall call my troops and property from the imperial camp and place them in your camp." Nadir Shah agreed, and it was done. [Harcharan.]

This plot took some time to mature. In the meanwhile, the Nizam had paid a second visit to the Persian king on the 18th and the Persian Wazir had been feasted in the Nizam's tent the day after. [Chron,] Evidently these meetings were held for hastening the collection of the indemnity first agreed upon.

Nadir Imprisons the Emperor and Nobles

Nadir bided his time for striking his treacherous blow. His sure ally was famine. The agreement had been made on the 14th and verbally confirmed by the emperor on the 15th but as the money was not paid the investment of the imperial camp had continued. [Jahan, 354.] The condition of the vast population within this huge enclosure was most sad, as we can see vividly in the letter of the Mahratta envoy who was present there: "Five or six days passed and then no food could be had in the camp. Grain could not be procured even at six or seven rupees* the seer. The country was a desert, nothing could be had (from the neighbouring villages). For five days the men went without food.'' As early as the 19th, or only six days after the battle, the supply of ghee had become entirely exhausted in the camp. [Chronicle.]

* Anandram, however, says that the price of flour reached Rs. 4 a seer.

But there was no escape. The Qizibash cavalry patrolled the road to Dihli and cut down or carried into slavery all who left the Indian camp. The few who slipped through the cordon of the enemy's cavalry were murdered or robbed of their all by the peasantry on the way. [Ali Hazin.]

When famine and despair had thus seized the Mughal camp in their grip, Nadir Shah summoned the Nizam to discuss certain matters which had yet to be settled.

On Thursday, 22nd February, the Nizam in full reliance on the treaty made a week earlier and without any apprehension, went to the Persian camp, in response to Nadir's letter. When he reached Nadir Shah's anteroom, he was detained there. Nadir sent him a message demanding 20 krors of rupees as indemnity and 20,000 troopers to serve under the Persian banners as auxiliaries. Asaf Jah was thunder-struck. He pleaded for abatement, saying, "From the foundation of the Chaghtai dynasty up to now, 20 krors of rupees had never been amassed in the imperial treasury. Shah Jahan, with all his efforts had accumulated only 16 krors but the whole of it had been spent by Aurangzeb in his long wars in the Dakhin. At present even 50 Lakhs are not left in the Treasury."

Nadir replied in anger, "These false words will not do. So long as you do not agree to procure* the sum demanded by me, you cannot leave this place." So, the Nizam was detained a prisoner in the Persian camp that day and the next.

---

*Literally 'point out where the money is.

Nadir pressed the Nizam to write to the emperor to visit the Persian camp again. The Nizam protested, saying that no such term had been agreed to before. The Persian king, however, assured him that he did not mean to break his promise, he had only found it necessary to meet Muhammad Shah a second time. [Siyar, 1, 91,] 'The Nizam had no help but to write to his master, reporting the exact state of affairs.

The unexpected failure of the Nizam to return the previous night had already created anxiety and rumours of treachery among the Indians and now when the truth became known from this letter, consternation and a sense of utter helplessness seized the emperor's court and camp. The Wazir was the only great noble left at his side, and naturally Muhammad Shah turned to him for counsel, but he replied that he could do nothing in such a situation and that the emperor should act as he thought best. Muhammad Shah was perplexed in mind and overwhelmed with grief. Some of the younger nobles counselled resistance and one more appeal to arms before yielding himself up to certain captivity. But the Emperor knew that a further struggle would only lead to greater misery and ruin. He decided to go to Nadir, leaving it to God to work His will.

On Saturday, 24th February, the emperor started from his own camp, accompanied by Muhammad Ishaq and some eunuchs and personal servants (khawas) and a retinue of 2,000 cavalry only. The other nobles who wished to bear him company were kept back by him. Arrived in the Persian camp, he was, according to the report that reached the Mahratta envoy at Karnal, welcomed by none, but left for a long time alone and uncared for and at night joined by the Nizam and Saadat Khan. Then he alone was taken to Nadir's tent. With this visit of the emperor, as the Persian State Secretary rightly says, "The key for opening the whole Empire of Hindustan came into the hands of Nadir Shah." In fact, the emperor became a captive and a guard was placed over him. The nobles who had accompanied him or previously gone to the Persian camp were told to consider themselves under arrest and Nadir gained composure of mind, so far as the chance of any Indian resistance was concerned. [Anandram, 42, Raj.]

Next day, 25th February, the emperor's wives, children, servants, and furniture were taken away from Karnal, and he was lodged close to Nadir Shah's tents. The captive nobles also called to themselves their families and retinue from their former camp. Qamar-ud-din Khan, who was the last great noble in freedom, was carried by the Qizilbashes to their camp, along with the imperial artillery at Karnal. Persian official historian throws the veil of hypocrisy over this treacherous coup d'etat played by his master. He describes the incident in these words: "Out of respect for the honour of the august family of the Emperor, the tents for his residence and the screens for his harem were set up close to Nadir Shah's tents and Abdul Baqi Khan, one of the highest nobles of Persia was appointed with a party of soldiers to attend on Muhammad Shah everywhere and engage in doing the duties of hospitality to the guest." [Jahankusha, 354,]

It was proclaimed in the imperial camp that the minor officers who had not been taken to the Persian encampment and all the common soldiers and followers could either stay at Karnal or go back to Dihli and their homes as they liked. [Siyar Harcharan, Raj, vi.]

Great terror and bewilderment now fell on the Indian camp. They were sheep left without a single shepherd and surrounded by wolves. Even their last remaining chief, the Wazir, was now taken away from them. The road to Dihli was beset by roving bands of Qizilbashes who had now no fear of resistance and by the peasantry who had risen in insurrection at the fall of the Government which had so long kept order.* The vast camp broke up and everyone fled wherever he thought best but comparatively few effected their retreat in safety. [Siyar following Ali Hazin.]

*Hanway (ii. 369): Flying parties of the Persian army within forty miles round the [imperial] camp cut off not less than 14,000 Indian marauders.

Their condition is graphically described in the letter of one of these fugitives. The Mahratta ambassador at the Mughal Court, Babu Rao Malhar, had accompanied the Emperor from Dihli to Karnal with his own escort and property and stayed there through these days of growing alarm and anxiety. At last, on Sunday, the 25th, he felt that all was lost. Mustering courage, or in his own words, 'making a fort of his breast,' he issued from the camp at about 3 o'clock in the afternoon. His elephants, camels, infantry and baggage and tents were sent towards Dihli by the royal highway, while he himself left it and plunged into the jungle for greater safety. Here he passed the night. Next day after riding some 80 miles along circuitous by-paths he regained the road near the Imperial capital. Saadat Khan was coming along this highway with a strong Persian escort and behind them the Mahratta envoy reached Dihli on the 27th. But that capital was no longer a safe abode. So, he left it that very day and halted for the night at Muhammad Khan's Sarai, some six miles south of the city. Thence, by way of Suraj Mal Jat's camp he reached Jaipur (on 6th March) without once halting on the way, and there he joined his colleague Dhondo Pant. His elephants and camels came, more slowly, from Dihli to Rewari. His feelings can be judged from his exclamation: ''God has averted a great danger from me and enabled me to escape with honour! The Chaghtai Empire is gone, the Irani Empire has commenced. Remain there in great caution!" [Rajwade, vi., No. 131.]

CHAPTER III

NADIR SHAH IN DIHLI: HIS RETURN STATE OF DIHLI CITY AFTER THE EMPEROR'S DEFEAT

The people of Dihli had been as careless of the outer world as the imperial Court. They had not at first realized the character of the Persian menace, nor the genius of the upstart shepherd-brigand who was approaching their country,' Confidence in the wardens of the marches produced a false sense of security, which was heightened by the magnificent display of the assembled forces of the three highest nobles sent from the capital on 2nd December 1738. When, on 19th January 1739, the secretary Anandram reached Dihli a day after the emperor's departure to join the army, he found that everyone, great and small, in the city had set his heart on accompanying the expedition. Some looked upon it as an opportunity for seeing the Punjab, others thought that a victory would be gained near the city and that they would return home very soon.

Then came the truth with starling suddenness. Early on the 15th of February, news arrived at Dihli that two days earlier the enemy's forces had triumphed, the two largest divisions of the imperial army with their generals had been killed or captured and the emperor's camp invested. The population of Dihli was cosmopolitan and included a large miscellaneous body ever ready to engage in violence and plunder. The Gujars or pastoral brigands lived in the close vicinity of the city and might be expected to raid its rich bazars whenever they heard that the imperial authority was paralysed or temporarily weakened. [Imad. 66.]

But Haji Fulad Khan the police prefect of Dihli, was a wise and energetic man. He kept the city safe by watching the streets day and night, and promptly pounced upon every creator of mischief. In the meantime, the highways leading from the city were totally closed by robbers; life and property became insecure outside the walls. Private individuals like Anandram who lived beyond the fortified town hired armed retainers to guard their houses, barricaded the ends of their streets and laid in stores of powder and shot for the defence of their homes and families. Twelve days passed in this kind of anxious watch, when on 27th February Saadat Khan arrived with 4,000 troopers and the lawless people were overawed. [Anandram, 38-41.]

The day after he had secured the Emperor's person, Nadir Shah despatched to Dihli Saadat Khan as the Emperor's representative and Tahmasp Khan Jalair as his own plenipotentiary agent with 4,000 cavalry to take possession of the city and palace for the victor and make arrangements for keeping order, so that no part of the imperial property might be plundered or secreted during the change of masters and the necessary preparations might be made for receiving Nadir in the palace. The two nobles reached Dihli on 27th February. They brought two letters from Muhammad Shah and Nadir to Lutf-ullah Khan, the governor of the city. The emperor ordered him to hand over to Tahmasp the keys of the palaces and imperial treasuries and stores and to guard the princes carefully. Nadir's letter praised Lutf-ullah for his honesty and devotion to his master and confirmed him in the government of Dihli on his own behalf.

Lutf-ullah Khan had talked of digging trenches round Dihli and making a defence. Therefore, Saadat Khan halted one march outside the city and wrote to Lutf-ullah advising him to make a peaceful surrender. Resistance was hopeless and the governor yielded up the city to the agent of Persia. [Shakir.]

When the news of the occupation of Dihli reached the camp outside Karnal the two kings set out on 1st March. Muhammad Shah rode an arrow's fight behind Nadir, as courtesy required. The emperor was accompanied* by only 1,000 horse and his Wazir by 10,000. The rest of the imperial army had dispersed to their homes immediately after the order of 25th February.

---

* Harcharan. Chronicle, But Hanway (ii. 373) gives a different description of Nadir's march to Dihli with 3,50,000 men, forming a column 12 miles long and 3 miles broad.

Nadir Shah and the Emperor enter Dihli Palace

The royal party arrived near the Shalimar Garden north of Dihli on 7th March, Saadat Khan had advanced from the city a day earlier to welcome Nadir. On the 7th Lutf-ullah went to the garden to wait on his master, who presented him to Nadir. The Persian king expressed great pleasure at Lutf-ullah's ready obedience and taking off a costly coat from his own person invested the Khan with it with his own hands. [Shakir.] Nadir and his army halted in the garden on the 8th, while Muhammad Shah went into the city to prepare the palace for receiving his august guest.

The fallen descendant of Babar and Akbar rode into his capital on a portable throne (takht-i-rawan) in silence and humility; no band played, and no banners were carried before him. [Chronicle,] A few nobles accompanied him, Ishaq Khan, Bahroz Khan and Jawid Khan.

Next morning, Friday the 9th of March, the conqueror entered Dihli riding a grey charger. His troops lined the road from the limits of the Shalimar Garden to the gate of the fort-palace of Dihli. The emperor welcomed his conqueror, spread the richest carpets, cloth of gold and other rare stuffs on the ground for him to set his foot upon (pa-andazi). Nadir Shah occupied Shah Jahan's own palace-chambers near the Diwan-i-khas, while Muhammad Shah lodged near the deorhi of the Asad Burj. [Anandram.] On this day the emperor acted as the host and placed dinner before Nadir, The Persian army encamped, some round the fort, some on the bank of the Jamuna near the city and some were quartered in houses throughout the city. [Ali Hazin, Jahankusha, 355,]

Saadat Khan had been in attendance on Nadir the whole of this day. At night he was severely reprimanded by the Persian king for his failure to raise the promised ransom and was threatened with personal chastisement if he did not carry out his word soon. It was too much for him. He retired to his own house and took poison.

The feast of Id-uz-zuha fell on Saturday, 10th March. In the morning the name and titles of Nadir were proclaimed as sovereign from the pulpits of the Jama Masjid and other places of prayer. [Siyar, i,, 98.] In the afternoon Nadir went on a return visit to Muhammad Shah's chambers and proceeded to his real business, the exaction of ransom. A little scene was now placed in order to throw a veil of outward decency over the pre-arranged act of spoliation. We can easily detect the truth in reading between the lines of the following diplomatic narrative of the Persian king's secretary. [Johankusha 355];

"Nadir Shah graciously remarked that the throne of Hindustan would be left to Muhammad Shah, in the terms of the agreement made on the first day and that the emperor would enjoy the support and friendship of the Persian monarch because both were of the same Turkoman stock.

''Muhammad Shah bowed low in gratitude and gave profuse thanks to the victor for his generosity. He had received no small favour; —it was the gift of a crown added to the gift of life. As a mark of his gratitude, he laid before Nadir Shah the accumulated treasures, stores, and rare possessions of the rulers of Dihli as presents to Nadir and offerings for his health (nisar). But the gracious sovereign of Persia refused to take any of these things, though the piled-up wealth of all the other kings of the world did not amount to a tenth part of a tenth part this immense hoard. At last, he yielded to the importunity of Muhammad Shah and appointed trusty officers to take delivery of the money and other property."

Dihli populace rise against the Persians.

While this peaceful meeting was being held in the palace, a scene of the opposite character opened in the city. Nadir's soldiers and camp-followers, mostly Turks, Kurds, and Mongols were wandering carelessly through the streets and bazars of Dihli as their king was in possession of the city. Suddenly about four o'clock in the evening (Saturday, 10th March) some idle talkers and mischief-makers started the rumour that Nadir Shah had been treacherously shot dead at the instigation of Muhammad Shah, by a Qalmaq woman-guard of the palace when he was returning from his visit to the Emperor.* [Anandram 44, Siyar, i , 98]

---

* This was a familiar stage-device of the storytellers of Dihli. The captive Shah Jahan was said to have formed a similar plot against Aurangzeb in Agra fort. Details of the alleged murder of Nadir Shah varied in the popular mouth. The following rumour reached Aurangabad, as we find in a Mahratti newsletter [Raj. vi, No. 134]: - "Nadir Shah, breaking his oath, faithlessly imprisoned the emperor and his nobles though the Pathans, who has joined him urged him not to do it. At the time of Nadir's entrance into Dihli there was a rising of the Pathans round him. Qasim khan Pathan and his brother, who were waving peacock feather fans over Nadir and his Wazir on their howdas, slow both of them with their dagger at the gate."

As all had heard that Nadir would go to the emperor's quarters that day, the story found ready belief. None cared to verify the news by a visit to the palace, though its gate was open, and people were passing in and out of it on business. [Al Hazin.] The rumour spread like wildfire and soon afterwards the hooligans and low people of the city armed themselves and began to attack the Persian soldiers and followers who were strolling through the streets alone or in groups of two and three. Their small number, their ignorance of the local language, and their unfamiliarity with the byways of the city put them at a disadvantage and they were slain. The rumour of the murder of their chief took the heart out of the Persians and they could not make any organized stand. The rising spread with the success of the rioters and the weak defence of the Persians. All night the murderous attack raged; it slackened after 3 o'clock next morning (no doubt owing to the exhaustion of the fighters), but revived with new energy at daybreak, which was the 13th bright lunar day of Falgun or the commencement of the Holi festival, when the low.er classes of Hindus are particularly excited and often intoxicated. [Chronicle and Raj. vi, 131.]

Among the authorities, Harcharandas alone says that the citizens rose in tumult when they were driven to desperation by the violent attacks of the Persian soldiers on their property and women. This statement goes against the probabilities of the case, because the time was only one day after Nadir's arrival, when the amount of the ransom and the manner of levying it were still being discussed, and Nadir was not the man to allow a premature fleecing of the citizen or relax the discipline of his army in a foreign town. All other writers represent the Indian mob as the aggressors. The higher classes and all good men held aloof; but they took no active step to pacify or control the hooligans, because the old Government agency for maintaining order had been dissolved; the gentry were too much divided by caste, creed, race and profession to combine and organize a voluntary police at a moment's notice, and their centralized autocratic Government had not developed their powers of initiative and self-help by giving them any opportunity of corporate action and municipal self-government.

Hanway heard what seems to me to have been the most probable account of the origin of the riot, namely that Tahmasp Khan sent several Persian mounted military police (nasaqchi) to the granaries of the Paharganj ward, ordering them to be opened and the price of corn fixed that the corn-dealers not being satisfied with the rate, a mob assembled; Sayyid Niaz Khan and several other persons of distinction put themselves at their head and slew the Persian horsemen and then the report was spread that Nadir had been murdered, which increased the tumult. [ii, 375]

According to Ali Hazin, seven thousand Persians were slain that night. But Abdul Karim gives the more probable figure of 3,000.*

* Ali Hazin says that some of the Indian nobles who had begged from Nadir Qizilbash guards for their mansions gave them up to the mob to be slain and even killed them with their own hands. But Abdul Karim tells the more probable tale that these guards were preserved, and their presence saved those houses from the vengeance of Nadir's soldiery in the next day's massacre and even the poor householders in their neighbourhood escaped sack by appealing to them.

When early in the night the first reports of the attacks on his soldiers were brought to Nadir, he refused to credit them and censured the complainants by saying that the wretches in his army had brought this false charge against the citizens in the hope of getting from him an order to plunder and slay them and thus satisfy their wicked greed. But the reports persisted and gradually became more alarming. He now sent out a sergeant to find out the true facts. The man, on leaving the fort-gate, was killed by the mob. A second agent suffered the same fate. Then the Persian king ordered a thousand musketeers to enter the streets and disperse the mob. But by this time the disturbance had spread over too large an area for these few men to succeed in quelling it.

On learning this, Nadir ordered that his soldiers should remain collected in their respective posts for the rest of the night, without spreading out or sallying forth to punish the Indians. They were not even to fight unless their posts were attacked. The gates of the wards of the city were watched by strong Persian pickets and the rioting bands were isolated in their respective quarters and prevented from combining or marching elsewhere. [Jahankusha, 357; Harcharan, Bayan 46-47; Ali Hazin, 298-299; Anandram, 44.]

Nadir's Massacre at Dihli

At sunrise on Sunday 11th March, the tumult broke out afresh. Nadir dressed himself in armour, mounted his horse and girt around by spearmen carrying daggers also, rode to the Golden Mosque of Roshan-ud-daulah in the middle of Chandni Chawk, opposite the Police Station and close to the Jewel Market. There he ascertained from which wards and classes of men the crimes of the night before had proceeded and then unsheathed his sword as a signal for the general massacre of the people of those wards.

His soldiers had so long held their hands back from retaliation solely in obedience to his command. They now hastened with drawn swords to wreak vengeance. Within the doomed areas, the houses were looted, all the men killed without regard for age and all the women dragged into slavery. * The destroyers set fire to many houses and several of their victims, both dead and wounded, Hindus and Muhammadans, were indiscriminately burnt together. [Jahankusha, 357-358.]

* Hanway (ii. 376)—Many refugees from the neighbouring country, joined by jewellers, moneychangers, and rich shopkeepers, headed by the Court physician, took arms in desperation, assembled in a body, and fought bravely for some time; but being so little accustomed to the use of arms, only died sword in hand.

The slaughter began about 9 o'clock in the morning and raged unchecked till about 2 P.M. Then Muhammad Shah in utter humility sent his highest nobles, the Nizam, and the Wazir, to beg the victor to abate his anger and pardon his erring subjects. [Jahan, 359.] Nadir listened to the prayer because he took no pleasure in wanton bloodshed and had only ordered the massacre as a measure of self-defence in imaginary fear of a universal rising of the Indian population. [Harcharan.]

The Kotwal was commanded to go through the city with the heralds of the Persian army, proclaiming to the men to cease their work of slaughter. They immediately obeyed.

Anandram (who was present in the Wakilpura suburb throughout Nadir's stay in Dihli) says that the houses in the Chandni Chawk, the Fruit-market Square, the Dariba Bazar and the region round the Jama Masjid were sacked. Harcharandas, too, speaks of only 2 or 3 mahallas near the Fort and the grain-dealers mahalla

(Paharganj) which was at a distance from it, suffering havoc. Abdul Karim defines the portion of the city subjected to massacre and plunder, as extending from the fort-gate westwards to the old Id-gah, northwards to the wood market, southwards to outside the Dihli gate in the city-wall. In addition to this area, "in Paharganj where the rising had started, many men were arrested on the suspicion of having caused the tumult and they were brought and beheaded on the bank of the Jamuna." [Bayan.]

The number of persons slain was found on a subsequent investigation by the Kotwal, to be 8,000 according to my MS. of Abdul Karim's memoirs, but the copy of the same work used by Sir U, Elliot's translator, Lt. Prichard, reads 20,000. The Persian State Secretary has 30,000 and the Maharatti newsletters (based on distant hearsay) give the number of the victims as 50,000 in one place and 3 or 4 lakhs in another. Harcharandas has one lakh; Hanway adds ten thousand to this last figure and says that 10,000 more committed suicide by throwing themselves into wells. [ii. 376.] All these are popular exaggerations due to distant bazar rumours. Considering the small area affected and the short duration of the havoc, 20,000 is the most probable number of those put to the sword.

We are told by more than one authority that many respectable Indian householders slew their own wives and daughters to save them from dishonour by the Qizilbash soldiery and then rushed on the enemy's swords or cut their own throats. Many women drowned themselves in the wells of their houses to escape a shame worse than death. But many more were outraged and dragged away as captives, though according to the Persian State Secretary, Nadir afterwards ordered them to be restored to their families. [Hanway; Jahan. 359; Rajwade, vi, Nos. 133 and 167.]

During the night of the rising two Indian nobles named Sayyid Niaz Khan (the son-in-law of the Wazir) and Shah Nawaz Khan, with Rai Bhan had attacked the elephant stables of Nadir, killed his superintendent of mahuts and taken away the elephants. They had afterwards shut themselves up in a fort outside the city and resisted capture. Azim-ullah Khan and Fulad Khan were now sent by the emperor to arrest them. They were produced before Nadir with 470 of their armed followers and were put to death by his order. [Jahan, 359.] Abdul Karim, however, holds them innocent of participation in the night's riot but says that they had merely shot down a number of Qizilbash assailants in the defence of their property and family honour during the massacre. All other authorities represent these two nobles as aggressors. Hanway had a different version of this incident. According to him [ii, 377] before the massacre of Dihli a party of the Persian forces had been sent to seize the cannon at the palace of an Indian lord.

n treacherously set upon and murdered by a body of Tartar [ughalpura]. Nadir sent a large detachment who fell upon these aughtered nearly 6,000 of them. The Persians brought away the ;ether with 300 persons of the chief rank among them, who were beheadeu, ... d their bodies thrown away on the sand bank (reti) of the Jamuna.

For some days after the massacre the streets of the doomed quarters of Dihli became impassable from the stench of the corpses filling the houses, wells, and roadside, none venturing to approach them in fear. At last, the Kotwal took Nadir's permission and had the bodies collected on the roads and other open spaces and burnt them. [Anandram, 50; Alji Hazin, 300.]

After the massacre Nadir ordered the granaries to be sealed up and guards set over them. He also set several parties of cavalry to invest the city and prevent ingress and egress. The city was in a state of siege; the roads were entirely closed. A famine broke out among the survivors of the massacre. Those who tried to leave Dihli and go to the neighbouring villages in quest of food were intercepted by the cavalry patrols, deprived of their noses and cars, and driven back into the city. After some days a lamenting deputation waited on the Persian king and he at last permitted them to go to Faridabad to buy provisions. [Hanway, ii, 377-378; Raj wade, vi, No, 133.]

But even the villages were no safer. The Persians marauded for 30 or 40 miles round the capital, plundering the villages, laying the fields waste, and killing the inhabitants who resisted. After the battle of Karnal a body of Persians had been sent to raid Thanesar, which they plundered, slaying many. During the Shah's advance to Dihli early in March, Panipat, Sonepat and other towns lying on the way were sacked.

[Hanway, ii, 384, 372-373.]

Exaction of Ransom from Dihli

Nadir spent two months in Dihli, secure in the occupation of the capital and engaged in the collection of the huge indemnity. On 26th March his younger son Mirza Nasr-ullah was married to an imperial Princess, a daughter of Dawar Bakhsh, * the grandson of Murad and great grandson of Shah Jahan. For one week before the ceremony, rejoicings on a grand scale continued day and night. The bank of the Jamuna opposite the Diwan-i-Khas was illuminated with lamps every night, while combats of elephants, oxen, tigers, and deer were held in the day.

* **Dawar Bakhsh's mother was a daughter of Aurangzeb.**

The conqueror allowed himself some relaxation after his arduous campaigns. Dances and songs were performed before him. One Indian dancing-girl named Nur Bai so highly fascinated him by her musical powers and ode in honour of him that he ordered her to be paid Rs. 4,000 and taken to Persia in his train it was with the greatest difficulty that she could save herself from this last mark of his favour. [Bayan, 56.]

The total indemnity secured by Nadir Shah at Dihli is estimated by his secretary at nearly 15 krors of rupees in cash, besides a vast amount in jewels, clothing, furniture, and other things from the imperial storehouses. The above figure includes whatever was taken from the nobles far and near and the imperial treasuries. [Jahan 361,] The grand total from all sources is raised to 70 krors by Frazer, according to the following estimate, which is clearly an exaggeration, as the State Secretary's figures are of the highest authority: —

Gold and silver plate and cash … … … 30 krors

Jewels … … … … … 25 kros„

The Peacock Throne and nine other thrones, also several weapons and utensils, all

garnished with precious stones … … … 9 kros „

Rich manufactures … … … … 2 kros „

Cannon, stores, furniture …' … … 4 kros„

Total … 70 krors

In addition to these, 300 elephants, 10,000 horses and the same number of camels were taken away. [Hanway, 383, 389.] Anandram, who was attached to the Indian Wazir, however, gives—sixty lakhs of rupees and some thousand gold coins, nearly one kror of rupees worth of gold-ware, nearly 50 kror, worth of jewels, most of them unrivalled in the world; the above included the Peacock Throne, [Anandram, 51]

The emperor had to surrender all his crown-jewels, including the famous diamond Koh-i-nur and the Peacock Throne of Shah Jahan which had cost 2 krors of rupees. In the public treasuries were found three krors of rupees but in the inner valuts, which had been shut during many reigns, a much larger amount was discovered. [Hanway, 383.] Abdul Karim says that the personal property of the Begams of Dihli was not robbed. This statement cannot be accepted, though it is fact that no torture was applied to these ladies or their servants for their jewels.

While the Emperor and the nobles were being squeezed of their wealth, the general public did not escape. A contribution of one-half of their property was fixed on all the well-to-do citizens who had escaped the massacre and sack, and a total of two krors * was ordered to be raised from this source. [Shakir and Anandram] Anandram, who was assessed five lakhs and had a Persian military guard placed at his door to enforce payment, describes the method of extortion thus: —

''Accountants were appointed to levy the indemnity from the inhabitants, under the guidance of Tahmasp Khan Jalair. But in order to save the citizens from utter ruin, nobles of both the Governments were directed to supervise the assessment of the ransom in the law-court in the presence of the public. Footmen (piadas) of the Kotwal and nasaqchis (military police of Persia) were sent to take a census of the houses and prepare lists of the property in each and enforce the appearance of the citizens, so that the sum to be contributed by each individual might be in accordance with his means. Helpless people, high and low, rich, and poor were compelled day after day to attend at the law-court where they were kept from dawn to sunset and often till one prahar of night......Without ascertaining the truth, the calamnies of Mir Waris and Khwaja Rahmat-ullah were believed.... The lists were prepared. The contribution of the capital totalled two krors of rupees. The Shah appointed the Nizam, the Wazir, Azim-ullah Khan, Sarbuland Khan and Murtaza Khan to collect the money. The entire city was divided into five sections and lists of the different mahallas with the names of their inhabitants and the amount to be levied from each were given to these five nobles." [Anandram, 53.]

* Hanway, 383, says, "About the middle of April, four kror was extorted from the merchants and common people." But Anandram is a better authority.

After every citizen had been assessed his exact contribution pressure was put upon them to pay the amount. Delay or objection only led to insult and torture. The floors of the houses were dug up in search of buried treasure. [Rajwadevi,

133.] Anandram writes in his autobiography: 'In the two mahallas where the collection was entrusted to the Nizam and the Wazir, the people were treated humanely as the Wazir paid a great part of the money from his own chests. But in the other three mahallas, especially in that assigned to Sarbuland Khan (i.e., Anandram's own!) the sufferings of the people knew no bounds—Whole families were ruined. Many took poison and others stabbed themselves to death." [Anandram, 54.]

It is said that the Wazir Qamar-ud-din Khan was exposed in the sun and thus made to pay one kror of rupees plus jewels and elephants. His diwan Majlis Rai was assessed a large sum and delivered to Sarbuland Khan to be tortured. His ear was cut off in open darbar, and retiring home in the depth of disgrace he committed suicide on 8th April. The Court agent of the governor of Bengal was beaten and he took poison with his entire family. As Hanway says, no barbarities were left unpractised. The tax imposed was strictly exacted. What numbers destroyed themselves with their own hands...' [Hanway, ii, 382, Frazer 199, Ti-i-Mdi; Tilok Das.]

All this time Nadir lived at Dihli as king. Coins were issued and the public prayer read in his name as sovereign and the title of Shahan Shah ('king of kings') which the Mughal Emperors had borne was taken away from them and applied to him only. The governors of the provinces of India had to proclaim him as their suzerain and in some instances mint his coins in the provincial mints, Muhammad Shah lived in Dihli like a prisoner of state and his nobles in the same helpless and degraded condition.

The entire population of Persia shared their king's prosperity. The revenue of that kingdom was remitted for three years. The chiefs of the army were lavishly rewarded; the common soldiers received 18 months' pay together, one-third of which was their due arrears, one-third an advance and the remaining one-third a bounty. [Bayan, 53.] The camp-followers received Rs. 60 per head as salary and Rs. 1.00 as bounty. [Jahan, 361.]

At Dihli Nadir Shah talked of making a pilgrimage to the tomb of Shaikh Muin-ud-din Chishti at Ajmer. This journey was really intended for the spoliation of the Rajput States because Ajmer is in the heart of Rajputana. At the report of his intended movement, Sawai Jai Singh in alarm sent his family and those of his nobles to the mountain-fastness of Udaipur and remained alone at his capital ready to flee away at the first notice. Baji Rao the Peshwa, then at Burhanpur began to form plans for holding the line of the Chambal to prevent a Persian invasion of the Dakhin. [Rajwade, vi. —133 Brahmendra S. C, 42.]

Nadir's Departure from Dihli

Nearly two months having been thus passed at Dihli and the contribution collected, Nadir Shah held a grand Court on Tuesday, 1st May, to which he summoned the emperor and his nobility. These nobles about a hundred in number were presented with robes of honour, jewelled swords and daggers, horses, and other gifts. With his own hands he placed the crown of Hindustan on the head of Muhammad Shah and tied a jewelled sword round his waist.

The Emperor bowed low in gratitude and said, ''As the generosity of the Shahan Shah has made me a second time master of a crown and a throne and exalted me among the crowned heads of the world, I beg to offer as my tribute the provinces of my Empire west of the river Indus, from Kashmir to Sindh and in addition the subah of Tatha and the ports subordinate to it." Thus, the trans-Indus provinces and Afghanistan were finally lost to the heirs of Babar. A considerable territory east of the Indus had also been seized by Nadir by right of victory over the local subahdars before the battle of Karnal and his right to their revenue was not disputed, though they continued to be governed by Muhammad Shah's officers. The governor of Lahor now signed an agreement to send Nadir 20 lakhs of rupees a year on this account, to remove the reason for any Persian garrison being left east of the Indus.

At this darbar of 1st May, Nadir Shah urged all the nobles and officers of India to obey and please their Emperor. He also gave them and their master much valuable advice on the art of government and decreed that henceforth farmans should again issue on Muhammad Shah's behalf and the Khutba and coins should bear his name and title. Khutba and coinage in Nadir's name, after having been current in India for two months, were now discontinued. [Jahan,362.] On this day the Persian conqueror sent off four farmans of his own to Nasir Jang, Nasir-ul-daulah, Rajah Sahu and Baji Rao, urging them to respect the settlement he had made and to obey Muhammad Shah in future. [Jahan Kusha, 361-362, Rajwade vi, 167, Ali Hazin, 301, Bayan; 57, Anandram, 80-83.]

Then, laden with the plundered wealth of India and the accumulated treasures of eight generations of Emperors, he set out on his return home. From India he carried away 130 accountants familiar with the finances of the Mughal Empire, 300 masons, 200 blacksmiths, 200 carpenters and 100 stonecutters, to build a city like Dihli in Persia, some goldsmiths and boat-builders were also forced to accompany him. These artisans were supplied with horses and other necessary articles and promised a large pay and permission to return to India after three years. But a considerable number of them contrived to escape before he reached Lahor. [Hanway, ii, 389.]

On 5th May 1739, he left Dihli after a stay of 57 days. Making a short halt in the Shalimar Garden outside the city he marched by way of Narela to Sonepat, where he overtook his army. The peasants rose in his rear and plundered stragglers and the hindmost part of his baggage train. It is said that he lost 1,000 transport animals (camels, horses, and mules) before reaching Thanesar. In anger he ordered massacres here and at some other towns on the way. [Hanway, 391]

From Sarhind, he swerved aside to the right and proceeded along the foot of the Himalayas, crossing the upper courses of the five rivers of the Panjab which were bridged for him. This he did in order to avoid the blistering heat of summer. On 25th May he reached the Chinab at Akhnur, 42 miles north-east of Wazirabad.* By that time the river had been swollen by heavy rainfall in the hills. When only half the Persian army had crossed over, the bridge of boats broke from the strength of the current and 2,000 Persians were drowned. A long halt had to be made, while a search was made far and near for boats. The other half of the army was ferried over slowly in boats and rafts at Kaluwal. After thus losing 40 days, Nadir himself crossed the river last on 3rd July and resumed his march.

* I here follow Anandram. Mirza Mahdi's words are: "He encamped on the bank of the river Chinab known as Wazirabad." This may mean that the Chinab was known as the river of Wazirabad and not that the Persians crossed at the town of Wazirabad.

By this time the heat had become intolerable even along the foot of the hills. Zakariya Khan, the subahdar of Lahor and Multan had accompanied Nadir up to this point. He was now dismissed to his seat of government with many gifts and a recommendation for promotion addressed to his master. Nadir Shah had been pleased with his devotion and ability and asked him to name any favour that he liked. The Khan very nobly begged for the release of the Indian captives taken away from Dihli by the Persian army. These were now set free by Nadir's order, [M.U., ii, 106.] Then, by way of Hasan Abdal and the Khaibar Pass the Persians returned to Kabul. [Jahankusha, 363-365; Anandram, 83-98.]

His return march through the Panjab was molested by the Sikhs and Jats who rose in his rear and plundered a portion of his baggage. The immense booty that he carried away from India did not remain long in the royal treasury of Persia. Eight years after this invasion Nadir Shah was assassinated and in the troubled times that ensued his hoarded treasurers were plundered and dispersed. *

*The Peacock Throne consisted of a gold-plated frame capable of being taken to pieces, richly jewelled panels fitting into its eight sides and detachable pillars, steps, and roof. It used to be put together and placed in the darbar hall only at the anniversary of the royal coronation but at other times it was stowed away in loose parts. When these parts were looted, they were naturally dispersed to different quarters. The genuine Peacock Throne of Shah Jahan no longer exists anywhere in the world but a modern and cheap imitation of it, made by the later kings of Persia, is still preserved at Teheran.

State of India After Nadir's Departure

Nadir Shah's occupation of Dihli and massacre of its people carried men's memories 340 years back to a similar calamity at the hands of Timur. But there was a great difference between the results of these two foreign invasions. Timur left the State of Dihli as he had found it, impoverished no doubt but without any dismemberment. Nadir Shah, on the other hand annexed the trans-Indus provinces and the whole of Afghanistan and thus planted a strong foreign power constantly impinging on our western frontier Timur's destructive work and the threat of further invasion from his country ended with his life. But the Abdali and his dynasty continued Nadir's work in India as the heir to his Empire. With the Khaibar Pass and the Peshawar district in foreign hands, the Panjab became a starting point for fresh expeditions against Dihli.

Not only were Afghanistan and the modern N. W. Frontier Province ceded as the result of Nadir's invasion, but the Panjab too was soon afterwards lost. Throughout the second half of the 18th century. Ahmad Shah Abdali and his descendants who ruled over Kabul and Lahor, constantly threatened the peace of Dihli and even the eastern provinces of the Mughal Empire. Their least movements, their slightest public utterances were reported to Dihli and Lakhnau and sent a thrill of fear through these Indian Courts and caused anxiety and precautionary diversion of forces to their English protectors, Hastings, and Wellesley. The hardy and trained warriors of Central Asia and Afghanistan could have captured Dihli by a few days dash from Lahor.

The Panjab, as the defensive barrier of India proper on the west, passed out of the hands of the ruler of Dihli even before the Abdali annexed it. Before the coming of Nadir, this province had attained to much peace and prosperity as the result of Farrukh-siyar's successful extinction of the Sikh guru Banda and his followers, and later on the vigorous campaigns of Zakariya Khan against predatory local chiefs and rebels. He had also added to the wealth and beauty of the cities, as Anandram enthusiastically describes. But Nadir's invasion undid all this. The country was first sacked by the Persian soldiers under orders and then by the lawless natives. Everywhere robbery and murder took place; gangs of robbers closed the roads to trade and peaceful traffic; everyone fought everyone else. Utter desolation and disorder seized the province. The Sikhs began to assert themselves in ever-increasing strength, until, half-a-century later, they gained possession of the entire province. From the end of Muhammad Shah's reign, they became an ever-present thorn in the side of the Empire. In the second half of the 18th century, they used to make almost annual raids eastwards to the environs of Dihli, plundering, burning, massacring, and destroying all traces of cultivation and habitation with ferocious cruelty. Sarhind, Saharanpur, Meerut, Shahdera and even Hardwar suffered from their ravages. Peace, prosperity, and industry disappeared from the region north and west of the Mughal capital.

After Nadir's return, the Mahratta established themselves in the southern and western provinces of the Empire in absolute security. The Dihli sovereign had no force, no general left to offer them the least resistance. Emboldened by the helplessness of the central Government, Mahratta bands began to penetrate repeatedly to Orissa, south-eastern Bihar, and Bengal. The local governor was helpless against their hordes and the emperor could think of no other means of meeting this danger than by begging the Puna Mahrattas to drive the Nagpur Mahrattas out of Bengal.

We are told by the Indian historians that after the departure of Nadir, the Emperor called his ministers together and devoted himself to re-establishing the administration and restoring the finances. But we know from history that he did not succeed and that during the ten years that he reigned after Nadir's invasion, the Government grew weaker and weaker, and matters drifted as before.

Indeed, there was no reason why there should be a restoration of the imperial power and prestige, while the character of the emperor and his nobles continued to be as bad as before. The Nizam was the only able and honest adviser left but he was now an old man of 82 or 83 and in anticipation of his approaching death rebellion had broken out among his sons. His domestic troubles and anxieties drew him to the Dakhin and kept him busy there till his death. Thus, the Emperor could not profit by the Nizam's wisdom and experience, even if he were inclined to follow his counsels—which was not the case.

The governors of Oudh and the Dakhin had no help but to declare their independence-in practice, if not in name, —as the subahdar of Bengal had already done. The struggle for the wazirship at the capital-i.e.,, for the post of keeper of the puppet Emperor,—continued more bitterly than before; the factions among the nobility quarrelled and intrigued as hard as ever and finally after the death of Muhammad Shah (1748) they came to blows in the streets and pitched battles on the plains outside Dihli and the great anarchy, which is only another name for the history of the Mughal Empire in its last days began destined to be ended only by the foreign conquest of the imperial capital half of a century later.

LIST OF TITLES WITH ISBN NO.

ISBN	TITLE
9788194914129	1984
9789390575220	1984 & Animal Farm (2In1)
9789390575572	1984 & Animal Farm (2In1): The International Best-Selling Classics
9789390575848	35 Sonnets
9789390575329	A Clergyman's Daughter
9789390575923	A Study In Scarlet
9789390896097	A Tale Of Two Cities
9789390896837	Abide in Christ
9789390896202	Abraham Lincoln
9789390896912	Absolute Surrender
9789390896608	African American Classic Collection
9789390575305	Aldous Huxley: The Collected Works
9789390896141	An Autobiography of M. K. Gandhi
9789390575886	Animal Farm
9789390575619	Animal Farm & The Great Gatsby (2In1)
9789390575626	Animal Farm & We
9789390896158	Anna Karenina
9789390575534	Antic Hay
9789390896165	Antony & Cleopatra
9789390896172	As I Lay Dying
9789390896226	As You like it
9789390575671	At Your Command
9789390575350	Awakened Imagination
9789390575114	Be What You Wish
9789390896233	Believe In yourself
9789390896998	Best of Charles Darwin: The Origin of Species & Autobiography
9789390896684	Best Of Horror : Dracula And Frankenstein
9789390575503	Best Of Mark Twain (The Adventures of Tom Sawyer AND The Adventures of Huckleberry Finn)
9789390896769	Black History Collection
9789390575756	Brave New World, Animal Farm & 1984 (3in1)

9789390896240	Brother Karamzov
9789390575053	Bulleh Shah Poetry
9789390575725	Burmese Days
9789390896257	Bushido
9789390896066	Can't Hurt Me
9788194914112	Chanakya Neeti: With The Complete Sutras
9789390896042	Crime and Punishment
9789390575527	Crome Yellow
9789390575046	Down and Out in Paris and London
9789390896844	Dracula
9789390575442	Emersons Essays: The Complete First & Second Series (Self-Reliance & Other Essays)
9789390575749	Emma
9789390575817	Essential Tozer Collection - The Pursuit of God & The Purpose of Man
9789390896578	Fascism What It Is and How to Fight It
9789390575688	Feeling is the Secret
9789390575190	Five Lessons
9789390575954	Frankenstein
9789390575237	Franz Kafka: Collected Works
9789390575282	Franz Kafka: Short Stories
9789390575060	George Orwell Collected Works
9789390575077	George Orwell Essays
9789390575213	George Orwell Poems
9788194914150	Greatest Poetry Ever Written Vol 1
9788194914143	Greatest Poetry Ever Written Vol 1
9789390896301	Gulliver's Travel
9789390575961	Gunaho Ka Devta
9789390575893	H. P. Lovecraft Selected Stories Vol 1
9789390575978	H. P. Lovecraft Selected Stories Vol 2
9789390896059	Hamlet
9789390575022	His Last Bow: Some Reminiscences of Sherlock Holmes
9789390896134	History of Western Philosophy
9789390575121	Homage To Catalonia

9789390896219	How to develop self-confidence and Improve public Speaking
9789390896295	How to enjoy your life and your Job
9789390575633	How to own your own mind
9789390896318	How to read Human Nature
9789390896325	How to sell your way through the life
9789390896370	How to use the laws of mind
9789390896387	How to use the power of prayer
9789390896028	How to win friends & Influence People
9788194824176	How To Win Friends and Influence People
9789390896103	Humility The Beauty of Holiness
9789390896653	Imperialism the Highest Stage of Capitalism
9789390575084	In Our Time
9789390575169	In Our Time & Three Stories and Ten poems
9789390575145	James Allen: The Collected Works
9789390896189	Jesus Himself
9789390575480	Jo's Boys
9789390896394	Julius Caesar
9789390575404	Keep the Aspidistra Flying
9789390896400	Kidnapped
9789390896424	King Lear
9789390575824	Lady Susan
9789390896455	Law of Success
9789390896264	Lincoln The Unknown
9789390575565	Little Men
9789390575640	Little Women
9788194914174	Lost Horizon
9789390896462	Macbeth
9789390896929	Man Eaters of Kumaon
9789390896523	Man The Dwelling Place of God
9789390896349	Man The Dwelling Place of God
9789390575909	Mansfield Park
9788194914136	Manto Ki 25 Sarvshreshth Kahaniya
9789390896509	Marxism, Anarchism, Communism
9789390575664	Mathematical Principles of Natural Philosophy

9788194914198	Meditations
9789390575800	Mein Kampf
9789390575794	Memory How To Develop, Train, And Use It
9789390896486	Mind Power
9789390896585	Money
9789390575039	Mortal Coils
9789390575770	My Life and Work
9789390896035	Narrative of the Life of Frederick Douglass
9789390575152	Neville Goddard: The Collected Works
9789390575985	Northanger Abbey
9789390896530	Notes From Underground
9789390896547	Oliver Twist
9789390575459	On War
9789390575541	One, None and a Hundred Thousand
9789390896554	Othelo
9789390575435	Out Of This World
9789390575015	Persuasion
9789390575510	Prayer The Art Of Believing
9789390575091	Pride and Prejudice
9789390896561	Psychic Perception
9789390575381	Rabindranath Tagore - 5 Best Short Stories Vol 2
9789390575367	Rabindranath Tagore - Short Stories (Masters Collections Including The Childs Return)
9789390575374	Rabindranath Tagore 5 Best Short Stories Vol 1 (Including The Childs Return
9789390896622	Romeo & Juliet
9789390896127	Sanatana Dharma
9789390575596	Seedtime & Harvest
9789390896639	Selected Stories of Guy De Maupassant
9789390575206	Self-Reliance & Other Essays
9789390575176	Sense and Sensibility
9789390575299	Shyamchi Aai
9789390896738	Socialism Utopian and Scientific
9789390896646	Success Through a Positive Mental Attitude
9789390575428	The Adventures of Huckleberry Finn

9789390575183	The Adventures of Sherlock Holmes
9789390575343	The Adventures of Tom Sawyer
9789390896691	The Alchemy Of Happiness
9789390575862	The Art Of Public Speaking
9789390896288	The Autobiography Of Charles Darwin
9788194914181	The Best of Franz Kafka: The Metamorphosis & The Trial
9789390575008	The Call Of Cthulhu and Other Weird Tales
9789390575107	The Case-Book of Sherlock Holmes
9789390896110	The Castle Of Otranto
9789390896745	The Communist Manifesto
9789390575589	The Complete Fiction of H. P. Lovecraft
9789390575497	The Complete Works of Florence Scovel Shinn
9789390896820	The Conquest of Breard
9789390896813	The Diary of a Young Girl
9789390896332	The Diary of a Young Girl The Definitive Edition of the Worlds Most Famous Diary
9789390575701	The Great Gatsby, Animal Farm & 1984 (3In1)
9789390575312	The Greatest Works Of George Orwell (5 Books) Including 1984 & Non-Fiction
9789390575992	The Hound of Baskervilles
9789390896707	The Idiot
9789390896714	The Invisible Man
9789390575657	The Knowledge of the holy
9789390575558	The Law & the Promise
9789390896721	The Law Of Attraction
9789390896776	The Leader in you
9789390896363	The Life of Christ
9789390896196	The Man-Eating Leopard of Rudraprayag
9789390896783	The Master Key to Riches
9789390575268	The Memoirs Of Sherlock Holmes
9789390896479	The Midsummer Night's Dream
9789390575466	The Mill On The Floss
9789390896790	The Miracles of your mind
9789390896660	The Mutual Aid A Factor in Evolution
9789390896448	The Origin of Species

9789390896905	The Peter Kropotkin Anthology The Conquest of Bread & Mutual Aid A Factor of Evolution
9789390896806	The Picture of Dorian Gray
9789390896271	The Picture of Dorian Gray
9789390575275	The Power Of Awareness
9789390896356	The Power of Concentration
9788194824169	The Power of Positive Thinking
9789390575411	The Power of the Spoken Word
9788194914105	The Power Of Your Subconscious Mind
9789390896899	The Power of Your Subconscious Mind
9789390896417	The Principles of Communism
9789390575787	The Psychology Of Mans Possible Evolution
9789390896615	The Psychology of Salesmanship
9789390575732	The Pursuit of God
9789390575398	The Pursuit of Happiness
9789390896851	The Quick and Easy Way to effective Speaking
9789390575947	The Return Of Sherlock Holmes
9789390575138	The Road To Wigan Pier
9789390896981	The Root of the Righteous
9789390575855	The Science Of Being Well
9788194914167	The Science Of Getting Rich, The Science Of Being Great & The Science Of Being Well (3In1)
9789390896011	The Screwtape Letters
9789390896073	The Screwtape Letters
9789390575336	The Secret Door to Success
9789390575695	The Secret Of Imagining
9789390896868	The Secret Of Success
9789390896431	The Seven Last Words
9789390575930	The Sign of the Four
9789390896004	The Sonnets
9789390896516	The Souls of Black Folk
9789390896875	The Sound and The Fury
9789390575244	The State and Revolution
9789390896882	The Story of My Life
9789390896936	The Story Of Oriental Philosophy

9789390896752	The Strange Case of Dr. Jekyll and Mr. Hyde
9789390896943	The Tempest
9789390575916	The Valley Of Fear
9789390575879	The Wind in the willows
9789390896080	The Wind in the willows
9789390575763	Their eyes were watching gofd
9789390575831	Three Stories
9789390896950	Twelfth Night
9789390896592	Twelve Years a Slave
9789390896677	Up from Slavery
9789390896974	Value Price and Profit
9789390896967	Wake Up and Live
9789390896493	With Christ in the School of Prayer
9789390575602	Your Faith is Your Fortune
9789390575473	Your Infinite Power To Be Rich
9789390575251	Your Word is Your Wand
9789390575718	Youth
9789391316099	A Christmas Carol
9789391316105	A Doll's House
9789391316501	A Passage to India
9789391316709	A Portrait of the Artist as a Young Man
9789391316112	A Tale of Two Cities
9789391316747	A Tear and a Smile
9789391316167	Agnes Gray
9789391316174	Alice's Adventures in Wonderland
9789391316136	Anandamath
9789391316181	Anne Of Green Gables
9789391316754	Anthem
9789391316198	Around The World in 80 Days
9789391316013	As A Man Thinketh
9789391316242	Autobiography of a Yogi
9789391316266	Beyond Good and Evil
9789391316761	Bleak House
9789391316778	Chitra, a Play in One Act
9789391316310	David Copperfield

9789391316075	Demian
9789391316785	Dubliners
9789391316051	Favourite Tales from the Arabian Nights
9789391316235	Gitanjali
9789391316068	Gravity
9789391316150	Great Speeches of Abraham Lincoln
9789391316662	Guerilla Warfare
9789391316839	Kim
9789391316822	Mother
9789391316211	My Childhood
9789391316846	Nationalism
9789391316327	Oliver Twist
9789391316853	Pygmalion
9789391316334	Relativity: The Special and the General Theory
9789391316389	Scientific Healing Affirmation
9789391316341	Sons and Lovers
9789391316587	Tales from India
9789391316372	Tess of The D'Urbervilles
9789391316396	The Awakening and Selected Stories
9789391316402	The Bhagvad Gita
9789391316303	The Book of Enoch
9789391316228	The Canterville Ghost
9789391316907	The Dynamic Laws of Prosperity
9789391316006	The Great Gatsby
9789391316860	The Hungry Stones and Other Stories
9789391316433	The Idiot
9789391316440	The Importance of Being Earnest
9789391316297	The Light of Asia
9789391316914	The Madman His Parables and Poems
9789391316457	The Odyssey
9789391316921	The Picture of Dorian Gray
9789391316464	The Prince
9789391316938	The Prophet
9789391316945	The Republic
9789391316518	The Scarlet Letter

9789391316143	The Seven Laws of Teaching
9789391316525	The Story of My Experiments with Truth
9789391316532	The Tales of the Mother Goose
9789391316549	The Thirty Nine Steps
9789391316594	The Time Machine
9789391316600	The Turn of the Screw
9789391316983	The Upanishads
9789391316617	The Yellow Wallpaper
9789391316426	The Yoga Sutras of Patanjali
9789391316990	Ulysses
9789391316624	Utopia
9789391316679	Vanity Fair
9789391316020	What Is To Be Done
9789391316686	Within A Budding Grove
9789391316693	Women in Love